ALSO BY JESSIE PARKER

Amazon eBook series for Visual Artists:

Money Smarts for Visual Artists (Part A): Business Accounting Made Easy

Money Smarts for Visual Artists (Part B): What You Can and Can't Claim and How and Why

Money Smarts for Visual Artists (Part C): Demystifying the Audit: Your Rights, the Procedures, and How to Win Your Audit

Tax Smarts for Artists: Accounting Secrets, Surprises and Essentials

Paperback:

Money Smarts for Visual Artists: Accounting Secrets, Surprises, and Essentials (and the eBook by the same name), Second Edition

See end of the book for Author Bio

TAX

SMARTS

FOR

ARTISTS

****

TAX
SMARTS
FOR
ARTISTS

Accounting Secrets, Surprises and Essentials

Jessie Parker, B.F.A, B.Ed

Any trademarks, service marks, personal names or product names are the property of their respective owners, and are used only for reference. There is no implied sponsorship, affiliation, certification, approval, or endorsement if we use one of these terms. This book is not endorsed by Intuit, publisher of *QuickBooks®* software and *TurboTax®* software in Canada and/or other countries. All other trademarks are the property of their respective owners. The author does not get paid to recommend any software mentioned herein. She has no contractual arrangement with any software company.

Specifically, this book is based on **Canadian law**. The information herein may not be correct or suitable for use in any other country as the laws in those countries may, and likely will, vary from the laws in Canada. Therefore this book may not be suitable for use by permanent residents of any other country, except as reference for prospective emigrants to Canada. It is however useful for Canadians working abroad and taxed in Canada.

While this book is based on Canadian law, it should be noted that all countries where English is the main language and/or an official language are based on British law, even if that dates way back in history. Therefore much of the following will be familiar to residents and citizens of those countries. In fact most of the content can be used almost as is, with minor adjustments. If you live in an English speaking country other than Canada, (such as the USA) use this book as a *starting point* and check with your accountant re the details that might vary.

****

ACKNOWLEDGEMENTS

Thanks to my seminar students and fellow artists for inspiring the content of this book with their enthusiasm and many insightful and pertinent questions.

Also thanks to my accountant for his skillful, thoughtful and pertinent help on my own Audit Appeal which also inspired the book content and helped me to help others..

Table of Contents

Introduction

The concept for this book came from considering what I could do to help artists by **filling in the gaps** with what they need to know about financial matters: things that aren't usually covered in art training. This book is about how artists can get all they deserve, while keeping on the good side of the taxman. The info is from an artist's point of view and in plain English, *not* in account-ese or legalese. You are benefiting from my many years of experience, and things I learned the hard way, by leaning on me... This is your essential guidebook.

Presumably you are taking advantage of this book because...

You are a **self- employed** visual artist in any of the following fields:

> visual art in any medium including fine crafts, and commercial fields, film/video.

>music (instrumental and/or vocal),
>writing and/or music composition,
> the performing arts including acting, comedy, dance
and any combination of the above..

****

Part I

Getting
Started

Getting Started

Keeping Good Records

THE DAYS OF THE PROVERBIAL SHOEBOX stuffed with disorganized receipts is over. If you give such a thing to an accountant, remember you are paying them the big bucks to do what you could have easily done yourself. This could run to hundreds of dollars !

3

An *easy way to start* is to put your receipts into piles by month, use a paper clip to hold each month's receipts together, then put them into a large envelope (the size that will hold a full sheet of paper).

Depending on how much paperwork you have, you may be able to use 2 to 6 such envelopes. Put the months, year on the outside of each envelope (such as, Jan, Feb, Mar, 2012). Now you are ready to record your expenses, and revenues.

A note about thermal receipts: they fade in a year or 2 to white, effectively erasing themselves. You need readable receipts for the tax department. Hence you will need to scan or photocopy your thermals annually, while tracing the basic info in ink so you can provide the "original" plus the scan for audit if needed. More in The Audit Process chapter.

You don't need to do your records monthly, unless you really want to. Quarterly, or half- yearly is fine. Annually in time for taxes works too. It should only take an average of up to 2 hours per month, to keep your records, using *QuickBooks*®. More on that later in Part II.

The software nowadays is so simple, even a child could use it. Most of the thinking is done for you, and that includes the math, and corrections. All the categories are set up for you. You can also customize. The sales tax is calculated based on what province is entered. If you can data input you can do it.

My accounting DIY/do it yourself efforts started some decades ago when all we had was paper ledger books, working in pencil in case of errors, and doing long addition using my brain and/or an adding machine. No kidding.

The advent of the calculator was a godsend. Then, the personal computer and the software came along and the whole process became so much easier!

So, having learned the hard way, it is now possible for me to pass it all along to you from a very useful perspective.

The info here is based on *unincorporated artists*, which is the case for most artists. Generally you are referred to as a "sole proprietor", meaning you are a one person business. You would generally refer to yourself as the "owner" of the business.

To Incorporate or Not

THE INFO HERE IS BASED ON UNINCORPORATED artists, which is the case for most artists.

Some sculptors, musicians and writers are incorporated. The issue could also arise if as an artist your content is controversial which could put you at risk for a lawsuit. And it could make sense if there is a liability issue concerning your particular medium. (That is why sculptors who do public commissions often incorporate.)

Since a corporation is a separate entity/person, being incorporated would limit liability to the assets of the corporation, not to anything personal, thus protecting the family..

Some accountants say it makes no sense to be incorporated from a financial standpoint (to save tax) unless your net income is $50k net or more. Discuss with your accountant the pros and cons in your particular case. The corporate tax rate is lower than personal (15% in Canada). While this part of it is tempting, consider the other costs.

If you are incorporated, you can pay yourself a "salary" but remember that you must declare that amount as income for yourself as a "person". So you are really not saving any tax in most cases.

The accounting rules for incorporated are basically the same as for unincorporated, but with a few refinements. If you are incorporated, once you get the hang of the basics here, see an accountant re the differences. In that case, you will be using the "incorporated" version of the accounting and tax software, and you will likely need an accountant.

It is likely and often advisable that you will be required to be officially audited annually by the accounting firm.

Visual artists who incorporate could put the art and equipment in a separate corporation, while running the business out of another corporation .

In some cases, especially for musicians, it may be prudent to set up more than one corporation: such as one for the performance part and another for the management part of the business.

One thing to consider for the established visual artist in particular: All inventory of art works may be taxed as deemed disposition at least at the cost of production before the art can   transfer into the corporation. This could mean a large tax bill to the artist as an individual, and may make incorporation unpractical/too expensive for the visual artist who has accumulated a large inventory of art works.

This is based on the opinion of one accountant, so it may be wise to double check this point with other accountants who have dealt with incorporating visual artists in their practise.

It would appear that it is more practical for the visual artist who expects to produce a lot of valuable art to incorporate before they accumulate very much inventory (unsold art) if they decide that they may need to incorporate (especially for liability reasons).

There may be some *estate related advantages* to being incorporated especially if the business could be carried on indefinitely concerning ongoing sales of publications, printing of art editions and the like. Musical compositions (songs, operas, and orchestral works) could have a life of their own long past the demise of the composer.

Hence, whether the incorporation occurs during the life of the artist or via the estate of the artist as administered by the beneficiary, there may be advantages especially concerning control of your own intellectual property ongoing.

It is also possible for the intellectual property (copyright, trademarks) to be in a separate corporation, and does not of itself do any business.

You, the corporation, would generally appoint yourself, the person, as the "President" of the corporation. A "succession" can be set up to accommodate the demise of yourself and any others who may continue on in the business, with appropriate titles for them (as you presumed heirs).

Remember the corporation is a separate entity and so is outside of the estate and not referred to in the Will. It can therefore continue technically forever…

Also there are fees involved with getting incorporated and for the ongoing process over the years. The whole thing is a somewhat more complex affair than being a sole proprietor .

 DIY/do it yourself is not so practical for those who are incorporated. It may or may not be to your net advantage to be incorporated. It is a permanent change, not one you can undo easily, so consider carefully if you want to go this route.

Obviously all of the above would need considerable discussion, consideration, and exploration with your accountant and/or corporate lawyer before making any decisions.

 Also be aware that some accountants may advise incorporation as they well know there will be more money in it for them.

So if you feel "pushed" into this option, get a second opinion to be sure it is the right way for you to go. Remember it is very hard to undo, so it is a very serious decision.

_____

Sources of Income

You may have many sources of income which together count as your self-employed gross income for the year. Use the T2125 form in Canada. These may include contract work with no benefits, such as free-lance teaching, doing freelance seminars for artists and any self-employed income regardless of whether it relates directly to your art..

For *visual artists* income sources include: selling your fine art either yourself or receiving payments from your gallery, commercial art, graphic design, commercial photography assignments, stock photography and royalties for the use of your art/photography..

For musicians: your share of group projects such as you are a member of a band and you receive your share of the performance based on your union rate for your time, and solo performances.. And of course royalties on the sale of your music.

For Performers, Writers: fees for freelance events, fees for acting in drama/ dance events. And fees for any paid writing projects, free-lance copywriting, musical compositions, etc.

The list could go on and on. You get the idea. Whatever self-employed income you receive without any benefits is income you claim on your business tax forms.

It is perfectly fine to combine several sources of self-employed income into one business claim form. Think of it as various departments of one business. One example often given by accountants is the roofer who does snow plowing in winter.

The taxman prefers a separate business for every little income source. But the single business model is done all the time. It makes life simpler, easier, is practical, and there is lots of case law supporting that. Don't let them tell you otherwise.

Now what *if some of the income is international*? Are you still liable to pay tax on that? Of course you are. In Canada, you are taxed on your world income!

So royalties on your images or writings from publishers abroad, or performance fees for shows in other countries are taxed the same as if you earned that income in Canada.

In order to not be charged twice on that income (especially re USA), it may be wise to get an ITIN (International Tax Identification Number) from the USA. That will prevent you being taxed again by the USA on income you are taxed on in Canada.

American born artists who are now citizens of Canada, please note: you may still have to file a tax form for the USA even though you are now a Canadian citizen and have no income from the USA. Talk to an accountant who is familiar with all the complex ins and outs of the American system.

Visual artists who exhibit aboard need to get full information from Import/Export re the rules concerning sending their art abroad and return of same. Generally if your art is not for sale, that is fine, but if it is for sale, then duty may be owed even if the art does not sell. Reams of forms need to be filled out so as not to be taxed on return of the art. Check out procedures through CARFAC.

Also, *art grants* are taxed as "income". . As well, any *monetary prizes* for your art which are paid by an organization/institution which is not a registered charity are taxed as income. And deemed disposition on *gifts of your visual art* are taxed as income even if they are gifts to family.

Artists who receive disability benefits should check to see what limitations there may be on taxable income, so as not to negatively affect their eligibility as a disabled artist. It is better to confer with an accountant rather than government departments so that your concerns are dealt with in a confidential manner.

Intellectual Property for Artists

Intellectual Property is , in a way, the most valuable asset the artist owns, be it related to visual art, music, or writing. It is often a source of income as well , in the form of royalties.

For the most part artists are concerned with *copyright.* Copyright is simply the right to copy the art work for publication or sale of a copy of the art. The visual artist/writer/musician does not sell the copyright per se, only the use of the image/ sculpture/ written copy/ music.

The sale of the art work does not include the copyright nor the right to reproduce that art. If the art buyer reproduces the art without paying a royalty or at least getting permission in writing from the artist, then that is infringement of copyright and could result in a lawsuit against the person(s) infringing on the copyright..

The artist owns the copyright in Canada simply by virtue of creating the art work in any medium. However the copyright is more defendable in court if the copyright is registered with the federal government, a simple process involving a small fee.

Collections of works may be registered together, which lowers the overall cost. Many artists register whatever they produce annually or every few years. You don't send in the actual work, only digital images/text/musical score representing the work in its final form.

This can be done by saving the material on a CD/DVD. You can also send yourself a copy via registered mail. (Do *not* open it), so you could "prove" your copyright dates in court. Not as good as registering, but better than nothing.

When registering after the fact, be sure to indicate in the file names the date of completing the art (at least month and year).

Some people think *"royalty free"* (concerning photography) means they are "free" to use photographic images as they wish (generally online).. All that term actually means is the royalty fee is low and that the image can be "freely" used simultaneously by several entities. Use is *not free.*

The term "royalty free" is mostly used in connection with stock photography images found on stock image websites.

"*Rights Managed*" ,re stock photography, means that only one entity can use the image at a time and the amount of time is negotiated as part of the contract which sets out the cost depending mostly on the details of the usage.

Unauthorized use of fine artists' images found online is also infringement as above and can end in legal action against the offending party.

Artists, do be aware that by digitally signing the agreement with social media, you are allowing them unrestricted use of your images placed on social media without any legal recourse or remuneration.

It is always wise to use some sort of digital watermark or © sign on any art work and written material posted online to hopefully discourage any infringement of your copyright. Be careful what you post. Be sure to read that horrid long agreement before you "sign" as it is very heavily enforced.

The proper way to go is via the payment of a royalty fee for use of an image . Visual artists can negotiate this personally or have CARCC do it for them. *See list of arts organizations and unions.*

Copyright in all media lasts till 50 years from the death of the artist. After that it is in the public domain, meaning you can copy without paying a royalty fee. (But moral rights last forever.) Before the latest update of the copyright law in Canada in 2014 photography was the poor cousin and copyright of photographs only lasted till 50 years from the creation of the photo.

Famously, Karsh outlived his own copyright on his early works! Now all media are treated equally at long last, thanks in part to much lobbying by CARFAC over many years..

Trademark (™) is usually registered for a combination of words and an image, both involving special graphic design. TM can also be used for a company name, music title or terminology for an invention . There is a substantial fee, and the TM lasts for 15 years. It can apply back to first use even if registered later. The TM can be renewed with an additional fee.

Canadian Professional Arts Organizations

There are *professional organizations/unions* for all the various types of artists. They are useful for professional information, arts opportunities, pertinent seminars, help with international sales/performances, international work permits, receiving royalty payments, scales of union payment rates, professional gallery exhibition fees, professional standards of conduct/employment, etc.

Here is a partial list for Canada:

Visual Artists*: Canadian Artists Representation (**CARFAC**):*Negotiates re exhibition fees, legal issues, presents seminars, some free legal advice .

All senior artists: *Canadian Senior Artists' Resource Network (**CSARN**)* who run seminars for senior artists and help with issues concerning seniors who are artists.

Visual Artists*: Canadian Artists Representatives Copyright Collective (**CARCC**)* Sets fees for use of copyrighted visual art for the artist, and collects the fees, (taking a percentage of the fees charged).

Musicians: *Canadian Federation of Musicians (**CFM**)* Protects musicians with insurance, union rates , legal help, contract help, opportunity to sell music online through *GoPro Tunes*, etc.

Actors, Performers*: Alliance of Canadian Cinema, Television, Radio Artists (**ACTRA**).* Members include actors, models, singers, comedians, announcers, dancers, etc.. Concerns include equitable compensation, safe/reasonable workplace conditions, health benefits coverage; use of fees, royalties, residuals agreements.

Stage Performers: *Canadian Acting Equity Association (**CAEA**):* Includes services for stage actors, singers, dancers, choreographers, stage managers, opera. Concerns are working conditions, opportunities and health benefits.

Writers: *Writers Union of Canada (**WUC**):* includes writers of professionally published books. Concerns: literary awards, health plan, negotiating collective agreements and benefit plans, the artist's rights per tax law, and use of literary agents.

Musicians and Writers: *Society of Composers, Authors, Music Publishers of Canada (**SOCAN**),* sets fees for use of music and writings automatically for the artist.

For more information about the above, just Google them. There is lots of info online.

Personal vs. Business Expenses

IT IS WISE TO KEEP YOUR PERSONAL FINANCES *separate from your business expenses*: it is easier for keeping things straight, and the taxman likes it.

You should have a *bank account which is just for your business.* This does NOT need to have a business name on it, as long as you keep it just for business and are consistent about that..

Bank accounts that are "business" accounts incur larger fees and are optional for your purposes.

 If you are 60 or over, you may be able to find a "no fee" or lower fee account for the 60+ age depending on what bank you use, and depending on whether it is still available if you don't already have one. Such plans , if you are lucky enough to have one, will have no minimum deposit and no fees.

It is also very advisable to reserve at least *one credit card for your business only,* and not use it for anything else. If you happen to accidently use it for personal, just deal with that as "personal various" coming from "Owners Capital" category so your software will not see it as a business expense. More on that in Part II.

The taxman loves it when you have a separate credit card or two for business. For one thing, this shows the taxman that you are a "real" business. The card, however , does not need to be in a business name, as long as you consistently use it for business. It is the use that matters, not the name. Also, you will find that having all your business expenses together on one statement makes your accounting a whole lot easier.

Remember you need an official receipt for all expenses that you want to claim.. Cancelled cheques/checks *don't count*. All receipts need the address of vendor/organization , amount, sales tax, and item description in order to be allowed to be claimed.

Some artists are in the habit of paying cash for business purchases. Be very sure you get very good and full receipts if you do this, as that is your only proof for claiming. See Part II for more info.

Actually it is recommended to use your credit card, or in a pinch, a cheque/check for all business related purchases. This will make your life easier in the end as then you can compare two proofs for each transaction (the receipt and the credit card or bank statement).

Software for Your Accounting and Taxes

THE BEST SOFTWARE FOR GENERAL ACCOUNTING that I have come across, and the one I use is *QuickBooks®* from Intuit® It is easy, intuitive, and you don't need to know account-ese to do it.

It allows you to add in an item that you missed, and it will recalculate everything after that for you automatically. It also lets you correct mistakes and recalculates everything again. This alone saves you many hours of work.

QuickBooks® uses terms like *Money in* and *Money Out*. The accountant language is *"debit" and "credit"*. For each debit (Dr.) there is always and equal and opposite credit(Cr). In other words, every transaction has 2 sides, called "double entry".

For example:

1. You take $$$ out of the bank and spend it on supplies (out of bank (Cr), into supplies Dr.).

2. $$$ comes out of the Bank (Cr.) to pay your credit card bill (Dr.).

3. $$$ goes into Supplies (Dr.), out of Credit Card (Cr)

4. Someone pays you for a painting/ article/ musical composition/ dramatic scene, and you put it into the Bank (into Bank Dr.) and into Revenue (Cr).

You will get the hang of it as you use the software. However, if you are nervous about trying all this yourself, get a bookkeeper to help you set up your accounts and show you how to start. A half hour lesson is likely enough as it is really very easy.

Remember, the software does all the math and corrections: you only do the data entry…

Then, as you print out your ledgers (Supplies, Office Expenses, etc.) and reports to show your accountant (if you choose to have one), it will be easy to see if there are any problems with which you need help.

Adapting the software for artists: Most accounts, as set up by the software, are usable as is, and are already set up by default. But you can always add custom accounts (such as "Art Supplies", instead of, or in addition to "Supplies")

It is useful to include the line of the tax form in your country as part of the description ,so you know where to put the total when you go to do your tax return (such as "Art supplies ,line 8811" as per the Canadian Form 2125 which is used for Sole Proprietor Businesses).

You may find that AccPacc Simply Accounting® is overkill for artists, and not easy to customize for your specific needs. It is fine for more complex, businesses that have employees, and/or sell in many jurisdictions, provinces, countries and I used it with difficulty for many years.

But when it was time to upgrade, the new version did not lend itself to being suitably customized as needed, so I switched to *QuickBooks*® which is very easy and much, much better for my usage as an artist. For *QuickBooks*®, you only need the "Standard Easy Start" version. The upgrade versions are overkill for your needs.

That said, there may be other brands of software out there , so if you have something you like to use, stay with what suits you.

There is no need to upgrade *QuickBooks*® annually as it stays the same basically anyway, so you can do dates backwards indefinitely, in case you want to go back and do previous years. You can also go forward indefinitely so you can continue onward each year.

You would only need to upgrade when something major happens. It was necessary to upgrade when Ontario went to the HST sales tax system so that the sales tax calculations would be correct.

By the way, in Canada, the software only calculates the HST and GST, not the various HST rates for all the provinces. More on that later.

For taxes, the same company (Intuit®) does a great job on what used to be called *QuickTax®*, and is now known as *Turbo Tax®.* You will only need the Standard Unincorporated version   (unless you are incorporated, of course).

There are other brands of software , as well, for taxes and accounting, but not being familiar with them, the only software recommended here is that with which I have personal experience . And no, I do not sell any software nor do I get any reward for recommending anything.

How To
Find Errors

HOW WOULD YOU KNOW IF AN ERROR was made by your bookkeeper, accountant or yourself?

The most common errors are the result of fatigue. Garbage in, garbage out. I recommend not to do more than 3 to 5 hours on your accounts/taxes per day, as your head may get muzzy, and your eyes go wonky after a while.

The most common errors:

1. Transposed numbers: 19 vs 91, etc.

2. Decimal points: $970 vs $97, etc.

3. An item in twice

4. An item missing altogether

5. An item in the wrong category

6. Item with wrong month date/or wrong calendar year (no kidding, it happens !)

For the most part, all the above can be found or verified using your ledgers (Supplies list for the year, etc.) The first 3 types of errors are easy to spot, the last 3 more difficult. Check your receipts against anything you are not sure about, usually that will do it.

Just a thought: How on earth would an accountant who does *not* want to see your receipts know if you had any of these errors??? Some errors could be guessed at, but *none could be truly verified without seeing the original receipts.*

QuickBooks® is very easy to correct: just make the correction in the Journal, and bingo QB will recalculate everything for you. What used to take hours the old way, now takes seconds.

If you are using an accountant to do your books, do not be satisfied with just the income/expense statement. That is just totals, and you have no way to tell if there are any errors, nor even how you are really doing at your business.

Ask for every expense ledger that applies to you. Make sure that the right things are going into the right categories, as well as looking for the above types of errors. Also ask for ledgers for "Bank", "credit cards", and "cash". These will help you spot errors. Again, remember, you are legally required to approve all accounts, and so you are ultimately responsible for any errors.

Once you know what you can claim or not, you should have all the info you need to decide whether to DIY or DIY-with-a-side-of-advice from an accountant or bookkeeper.

To Use an Accountant or Not

ACCOUNTANTS ARE A VERY VALUABLE RESOURCE if you are earning sufficient revenue to *afford* one, that can be great for you.

But I often hear artists say, "Oh, I just hand my stuff over to my accountant and forget about it, I don't have time for all that". In other words, they just play ostrich with their heads in the sand, often with no understanding of what the accountant does.

But if there was an error, would you know it and could you find it? Just because the forms and accounts look nice and neat when printed out, does not mean there are no errors!

Could you find something that could be a problem and ask about it and understand the answer according to tax law?

Do you know what reports you need from your accountant in order to check things out? (Most will not give you many important reports unless *specifically asked for them* !)

See the previous chapter to nail down exactly how to find errors. Don't expect the accountant to find all of them. Sometimes they won't spot them all. You know your accounts better as you are the one spending the money, after all.

Even if you use an accountant, by the time you organize your records properly and check all the resulting printouts from the accountant, it would have taken very little more time to DIY!

Remember , ultimately, *you are responsible for checking everything and correcting anything needed. Using an accountant does NOT get you off the hook legally !*

If you do decide to have an accountant do your books for you, here is what you need in reports from your accountant:

All ledgers of expenses that you have (such as professional supplies, office expenses, advertising, travel, etc.) plus your credit cards, Bank, cash, any liabilities, and Revenue. (As you can see you need much more than just the Profit and Loss Summary .

That is quite a few statements, but you won't know for sure if there are errors unless you have all of them. Just the summary of income and expenses is not anywhere near enough. Also you would need to *compare the reports with your receipts...*

The services of an accountant is recommended for:

1. **General advice** and to clarify where unsure;

2. Getting news of any **changes in tax law** that would apply to you;

3. What to do about any **special situation** that is specific to you, like an **audit**

4. Double checking **to see if you fully understand** all you are doing with your books.

5. An **annual review meeting** where you review whatever you feel is needed.

Meeting with an accountant annually can be very valuable to keep you on track and avoid any potential future issues. Usually an hour will suffice if you are well organized. This is an excellent use of your money.

Why spend $1000's on something you can do yourself, which is mostly just data input, or for work that you could have a bookkeeper do?

The role of the accountant has evolved somewhat over the years, from basically a glorified bookkeeper back in the 60's and 70's to an important guide for your business today.

This is in the form of business strategy, advice, law updates, and forward planning for your business. Almost like a coach, but on the financial side of things, the accountant can be a very valuable member of your business team. Her services are a very wise use of both your time and the accountant's time and expertise.

If you believe you need help, however, consider these points:

As of this writing, bookkeepers charge $30 to $60 an hour, while accountants charge a lot more, often over $150. per hour.

Some bookkeepers will come to your home or office, and get you set up with your software, and some will even teach you how to DIY. Ask around.

Most of 'accounting' is just data entry, which you can do or a bookkeeper can do or an accountant can do. This is where a financial decision can be made.

If an accountant says, "Let's try this", or "you might get away with that", be very leery, as it usually means they don't know the answer (but won't admit that). If you end up in doo-doo over it, *it's on **your dime** to correct the situation*, (unless you can prove it was really the accountant's fault, in which case you may be able to get the accountant to cover the time it takes to make the correction)

They should have "Errors and Omissions Insurance" (called E&O insurance), same as Financial Planners and Lawyers do. Remember that even if an accountant gives you erroneous advice, you usually still have to pay the bill for it!

However remember that with E&O they can claim back the refund they pay you so they are not out of pocket to correct an error or to refund work done in error. That is what the insurance is for! There are many cases of artists having to pay hundreds of dollars even though the advice was completely useless or bogus (as proven with further advice from other accountants).

One criteria in choosing an accountant might be whether they have E&O or not!

Finding an accountant:

Someone who impresses you in a workshop, or in a networking group, or someone a friend knows and is happy with is a good place to start. It is good *to interview a few before deciding though*. This is a major decision.

CGA's (Certified General Accountants) generally work out of a home office, and are used to small businesses.

CA's (Chartered Accountant) generally work for larger firms, and hence charge somewhat more.

For your purposes, they both should have the knowledge and skills you need.

It is great if you can find an accountant specifically used to working with artists. If you can't, the info in this book will give you the background you need to DIY and/or to "train" your accountant...

What have you learned so far?

.You need to keep good records

.There are many sources of income for the artist

.There are many unions and organizations to help you as an artist

.You don't necessarily have to be incorporated

.You can use an accountant for advice without necessarily having him/her do your accounts and/or taxes (DIY with a side of advice)..

.Today's software can make your business life a lot easier . But be on the lookout for errors.

.You are legally responsible for any errors your bookkeeper/accountant makes.

MY NOTES

_____

_____

_____

_____

_____

_____

_____

_____

_____

_____

_____

_____

_____

_____

_____

_____

<u>MORE NOTES</u>

_____

_____

_____

_____

_____

_____

_____

_____

_____

_____

_____

_____

_____

_____

_____

_____

****

PART II

The Nitty
Gritty
Made Easy

****

The Nitty Gritty
Made Easy

What You Can
And Should Claim

ALL BUSINESSES CLAIM EXPENSES AND INCOME.
So do you as an artist, and yes, you *are* a business,
for tax purposes, even if you don't think of yourself
that way…

You are allowed to claim all expenses that are necessary to the running of your business. *It does not matter if you will be in the red on paper.*

In fact if you only claim some years and not others, this will ring red bells at the tax department, as they will assume rightly or wrongly that you are hiding something in the years that you did not claim. Consistency is king for accounting.

Some artists claim that they only need to file tax forms in years that they make a profit. Not so. In fact *unused losses* of any one year caused by Business Use of Home *carry forward* to other years**,** while *net losses* claim automatically against other income . So not claiming is literally leaving money on the table**.**

The time will come when you will be glad you have those old losses to claim against your profits in the good year that you make the big bucks. Remember, **the taxman expects and requires that you file every year***, whether you are in the red or in the black.*

Also, if you have income claimed on your general tax form, from say, salaried job(s), or pension, your loss will automatically claim against that in the year of the loss, saving you tax that year, and any unused loss will carry forward as a "non-capital" loss indefinitely until you decide you want to use it. It is literally "banked" for you. (No interest paid however.)

If you are doing the seniors income splitting (available in Canada) then that will, however, usually result in no carry forward as the loss will claim against the split income, saving tax in the current tax year, and often resulting in a tax refund.

If you did not claim for this year when you should have, is it too late? No, you can **back-claim** anytime going back up to 3 years as long as you owe no tax. Just do the self-employed business tax form (T2125 in Canada) yourself, one per taxation year not previously filed.

But if you have net income, not reported, you should contact an *accountant who will be able to back-claim for you* and do the special forms to claim amnesty. You *cannot* do this on your own. You will of course need proper receipts for all back claims. You will not be allowed to claim anything based on just verbal say-so..

The **amnesty procedure** will avoid penalties or at least lower them. You will usually still have to pay any accrued interest, though. So the longer you wait, the more you will owe in interest on your tax.

And they will keep a close eye on you hereafter.

You will, of course, have to have *receipts for all your claims* (though you don't need to send them in), so only claim what you have receipts for. Read all the info following re how to do everything before you start.

Before doing any back-claims, it will of course be necessary to do your accounts first, starting with the first (earliest) year you are claiming and going forward. Get help from a bookkeeper if you need it, to get it all sorted out.

Remember that your losses will result in refunds as the losses will claim against any other income (job, self-employed, pension) . Expect it to take 3 or more months for the taxman to redo your returns to generate what the refunds will be, and send you the money.

After this, **always file even if you have a loss**!

Remember if you don't file, you are paying more tax than you need to… losses are literally "money-in-the-bank".

If you have not been keeping your receipts, be sure to keep them from now on, so you don't lose out. Also keep in mind that any receipts that you may be able to request a duplicate for later could be claimed, as you could contact the vendor later if audited.

Note: All of following is based on Canadian tax forms, here the T2125. For other countries, the form name will be different but the general info will be the same or very similar.

By the way if you have a substantial bill in a taxation year for something you won't actually use till the next taxation year ,you can postpone claiming it till the year you use it. In the year incurred claim using Visa(etc.), and "personal various" so it won't "count". Then claim with the category and "cash" in the year actually used.

To summarize…

If you need to make a purchase in order to

***Produce or perform* your art,**

to ***store* it,**

***insure* it,**

***display* it,**

***ship* it,**

***market* it   or**

***research* it ,**

then you can claim it !

It is recommended that you obtain the Sole Proprietor tax forms (*the T2125 in Canada*) for the current year or last year, so that you can follow along .

Now let's look at some of the *specific things* that you can claim as an artist:

First: the *industry code* goes on first page of your self-employed/business tax form, which you use for claiming your expenses and revenue from your art and any other self- employed income (like part time teaching, commercial art, commercial or stock photography or graphic art/design).

Some useful industry codes in Canada are: visual artist: 711511; graphic designers: 541432; and photography services : 541920;writers,authors 711513; independent actors, comedians, performers 711512.There may also be others that could be appropriate for you. Search around Help in Turbo Tax (2014 or earlier) or other tax software. Use the code that is for your main creative activity.

It is OK to switch once from something else, but avoid switching back and forth year after year. The tax man likes consistency.

You would use Part I (*Business income*) for your gross revenue on the sales, commissions, fees line. (Professional income is for doctors, lawyers, and such which would not apply to you.)

Your total gross income will automatically show up at the bottom of the main first page.

Inventory Valuation:

If you are a visual artist, you do not need to use the Cost of Goods Sold section, as *visual artists in Canada are allowed to value their inventory at Nil,* so this section is irrelevant for you. This means that you will *not be taxed* on your unsold art annually.

That is one concession that the tax department has made for visual artists specifically since 1986, and saves lot of work. See Estate chapter for more.

If you were to claim your inventory at the cost of production, you would be required to pay tax on any unsold works annually, which could be a financial burden ongoing.

While there are advantages for the unincorporated visual artist, there may be repercussions for the unincorporated estate concerning the deemed disposition on death. See Epilogue section on estate issues at end of the book

If you have been valuing your inventory, and would like to switch to the Nil method, it is recommended to confer with an accountant as to the appropriate way to switch over to the inventory at Nil method.

Hobbyist vs. Professional Status:

If you have been considering yourself a hobbyist, hence not claiming expenses, and not filing and yet you are busy showing your visual art in venues where you can sell your work and where the exhibitors are assumed to be professional, then you are de-facto a "professional" to all intents and purposes and should proceed as such from that point onwards.

Professional venues include galleries that charge 35% or more, and trade shows that charge mid 3 figures to 4 figures for the art booth.

You will need to pay tax on any art sales income as outlined above (or remove your art from the professional venue) if you are in fact a hobbyist.

And if you have been collected widely (both your country and other countries) and/or take advantage of ongoing professional quality training, then you are proceeding in a professional manner.

You can't be both professional and amateur at the same time: decide and proceed accordingly. Trying to stay on the fence is like trying to swim with one foot on land and the other in the water. It doesn't work! You are in or you are out...

In fact, if your hobbyist income claimed and taxed as "other income" on your general tax form is substantial (over $5000,say) for several years, the taxman may look further and require you to officially set up a business and claim both income and expenses from then onward.

Why would they be so kind as to encourage you to claim your expenses? Well, there is that deemed disposition on death which will mean considerable tax re the art in your estate. See details in the Epilogue.

Types of Expenses, What They Mean, How to Deal with Them

THE "EXPENSES" SECTION OF THE T2125 TAX form (Canada) is where most of your expenses go so we will spend some detailed time on it.

(Note: If you are in the USA or other country your expenses may be different in some parts of your tax forms , and the sequence or exact language may be different, but most of the general categories will be very similar or the same. Ask your accountant to point out to you what the differences are.)

Although each line on the tax self-employed form (T2125 Canada) has a number, I will just be referring to the description of the expense. This form is used for all self-employed sole proprietor unincorporated businesses. Expenses that are never used by   artists are not referred to here. The expenses are presented here in the same sequence as on the Canadian business self-employed form.

>> *"Advertising"* is used for both **advertising and marketing**. This will include not just ads, and paid profiles in magazines and books, but also your brochures, bookmarks, postcards and any other *promotional items* you have printed.

Also included are fees for *visual art show booth rentals* plus all other attendant fees like electrical, internet, cleaning, etc. which may get added to the main show booth fee.

For *writers:* ads for your services in appropriate publications. For *musicians*: promos expenses for your performances/concerts for which you are personally responsible.

For *actors*: promo book with your promotional photos and reviews.

All of this is *marketing expense* as you are promoting yourself and selling your art, writing or performance skills.

 In addition this is where you could put fees for *networking events*, even though food may be provided to attendees. Again, this is under "advertising" because you are promoting yourself via these events, and you have to pay the fee even if you don't eat anything, and even if you do not attend. DO NOT put this under "meals".

>> ***"Meals and Entertainment"*** category is not used much by artists. This is mostly for local meals where you must buy your meal, such as at an arts related seminar that you attend.

The meals amount is reduced by 50% on the theory that you have to eat anyway. (Do this in the accounting software as an adjustment.) A good idea, when you finance a meal as a business expense, is to keep the receipt with the menu on it, and write on the back as to why the meal is being claimed.

Entertainment could include an event that you finance in order to get buyers of your art, such as a private showing of your visual art works. Be very careful not to overdo it on this.

Meals while on trips are under *travel* now.. See the Audit section for more.

>> *"Insurance":* This is mostly used for special insurance for your visual art in your studio (a rider on your general insurance).

If you have a rented or privately owned studio, and have to insure it, the insurance for that would also go here. It may be possible to add a suitable rider to your household insurance or as a separate business insurance for your home-based business. Inquire from your insurance agent.

Be sure to check re any municipal by-laws that may relate to operating a home-based business where liability could be an issue. Ask your accountant re details and how to research this without any repercussions.

Insurance for a *rented visual art expo show booth* would also go here (This is quite often a required expense, and is mostly for liability, as well as theft).It may be wise to bite the bullet and insure your art if you are having a solo visual show or a two-person show as there are many more works involved, and therefore somewhat more risk..

Visual Arts Organizations Insurance Requirements: Most visual arts organizations will have a disclaimer that says that the artist is advised to insure their work that is at a group exhibition. (Most artists don't, just taking a chance on it.) It can be very difficult to get any kind of reasonably priced insurance for art at group exhibitions due to the details changing for every show and not being predictable up front for a Blanket policy. Ask your insurance company (household) about this if this is an issue for you.

>> *"Interest":* this also includes *all bank charges,* including bank fees, Interac fees, PayPal charges, interest on a Line of Credit or other loan for your art production/expenses/equipment. "Interest" even includes exchange on the dollar (for USD to CAD, for instance).

>> *"Business tax, fees, dues, licenses, memberships"* This is for your visual art association membership dues, small visual art organization group exhibition fees, annual dues for networking groups, ACTRA dues, CARFAC annual dues, other professional dues , SOCAN fees, website hosting fees, domain name fees, copyright license fees related to your art activities and any fees that don't fit into advertising per se.

(Business tax should only be required if you rent a commercial location for your studio.)

>> *"Office expenses"*: This includes any expense or service except the above and travel and supplies. Such as, having framing done for you, photocopies, digital fees for services, software under $200, printing costs for visual art, etc.

Also here you could claim educational expenses that relate to your art practice, such as books, CD/DVD's, monthly access fees for educational services, generally referred to as "professional development" (unless you want a separate category under "Other", see below.).

Internet could only go here for a separately owned/rented studio with a separate internet account for the studio.

However for home studio, your general internet bill *cannot* be claimed here, as the taxman will NOT believe that it is only for business. See Business Use of Home for *how to claim Internet properly.*

Educational expense as *Professional Development* could be here or under "Other". Includes professional books, eBooks , courses, seminars continuing education in one's field.

More examples of non-visual art office expenses:

Musicians: software and instruments under $200 related to music business; CD/DVD's of sample performances. Tuxedo cleaning for band members.

Writers: Cost of producing samples of your writing for publishers/magazines.

Performers: cost of printing your "book" , CD/DVD's of sample performances.

>> *"Supplies"*: This is for anything that you can touch and see that is art and business related and that you are responsible for supplying from your own pocket..

Art supplies are anything used in the production by you of your visual art.

Visual art supplies include: paints, mediums, canvases, brushes, papers, inkjet inks, drawing tools (pencils, pens, pastels, etc.) ; cameras, and photography accessories under $200;.Framing items (frames, glass, backing, matts, hammer, brad inserter, pliers) labels , etc.

Musicians: supplies like reeds, musical score paper, polish for instruments, etc.
Performers: theatrical costumes, theatrical makeup if required to self-supply.
Writers: general office supplies (see below); port-folios of writing projects.
Dancers : ballerina/tap shoes, theatrical makeup, theatrical costumes where required to self- supply

All disciplines: General tangible office supplies include paper, envelopes, printer inks, pens, etc.

>> *"Legal, accounting, and other professional fees":* This is fees you pay your lawyer, accountant, etc. for their services to you related to your art business. This also includes your annual consultation with an accountant.

>> *"Rent":* You would use this only if you rent an art studio or office separate from your home.

>> *"Maintenance and Repairs":* This applies to your *rented* or separately owned studio/office space only. Such as blinds, special lighting for studio, special flooring, paint for walls, and for fixing leaks, etc. Do not use this line for the Business Use of Home (dealt with later) .

>> *"Salaries, wages ,benefits":* Wages could include model fees, someone you pay to help with framing, or producing a sculpture, or helping you at an art expo booth, or bookkeeping . These are generally casual labour, so you are not paying them employment benefits, since you are self-employed.

Writers may pay out business coach fees, *Actors* may pay acting coach fees. *Singers* may pay voice coach fees.

One caution here: If you hire and pay a relative or friend for an art-related service, you may claim the amount as expense here as long as it is "reasonable", that is, at or below what you would have to pay someone for the same work as a "pro". However it is *very* important that they claim the same amount as income (under "Other Income") on their tax forms. The taxman watches for this.

 If the income is not claimed a fine of up to $25,000 can be levied to the recipient of the casual labour pay (intended to discourage "under the table" labour.)

Therefore, it is wise and kind for you to inform your relative or friend about this as you could be saving them a huge penalty. Then if they choose to ignore your information, at least you did your duty, so then you are off the hook legally! How could they find out that this happened? Via an audit of your books! See the Audit section for more.

>> *"Property Tax"*: This only applies to a separate studio, not one in your home. (We will get to the home studio stuff later.)

>> *"Travel":*   (includes transportation, accommodation, 50% of meals while travelling) This is often a big category, and can cause troubles if not done correctly.

"Travel" includes air, train, bus, taxi, car rental, hotel, B&B, apartment by the day/week, etc. and 50% of your own meals (not meals for your family), and events involving travel which are specifically related to your art.

In general, Travel expense especially applies where travel is a recognized as a part of your business as an artist.

Tips on meals are theoretically "optional" so are not claimed at all or only claimed if charged as part of the paper bill. Be sure to keep the meal bill as your proof. Cash tips are not claimed as there is no proof. Remember, to claim anything, you need proof.

You can claim all your accommodation if it would cost the same if you were alone. If the accommodation is charged at so much per person, then only claim your portion. You should also adjust for how much of the trip was actually for business (a suitable percentage).

Visual Artists may need to travel to do their art, research for their art, show their art, and /or go on speaking tours concerning arts related topics.

Musicians often find travel a major expense where they must travel a show and cover their own expenses. Some expenses may be covered, others not. All of this needs to be spelled out clearly in your agreement with your venue manager to avoid misunderstandings.

Writers, especially travel writers, may be required to cover their own travel expenses. Some writers manage to get some coverage of costs from travel destinations like hotel/resorts/cruises but still must cover some of the expense. Free-lance journalists usually cover their own travel but may have "advances" which would be treated as income. Likewise authors on a book tour may have some expenses covered by the publisher but might be responsible for some expenses. Claim whatever is on your own dime.

Performers can claim whatever is out of pocket, especially if required to travel a play, etc.

Artists who claim all of what is actually a *vacation* for the family usually get caught. The taxman watches for that. More on that in the Audit section.

>> ***"Telephone and Utilities"*** :This is usually only used if you rent/own a separate studio and have the telephone/cell under a business name , and for hydro for the same studio *only* if it is billed separately. Not for Business Use of Home.

Therefore, you *may not claim your home phone, or cell phone for business, unless it is registered and invoiced as a separate business phone* . That likely would not be economically viable as the business phone in any case since the phone would then be at a higher rate, so there would actually be no savings for you. You may however claim long distance charges for business use. Best to keep a log of who and why for each call.

More about this in the Audit and "Business Use of Home" sections.

>> ***"Fuel costs"*** (except for Motor Vehicles) This is rarely used for artists. It could apply to a separate studio/office, such as heat for the rented space. (wood chips for a wood chip stove, etc.).

>> *"Delivery, freight, express"* applies to shipping costs of your art by post, bus, FedEx, UPS, both to and from any art show, gallery or art buyer, publisher, producer, director..

>> *"Vehicle expenses"* will pop in here from The Vehicle Chart . More on that later.

>> *"Capital Cost Allowance"* (from the Capital Cost Allowance chart): This will automatically pop in when you fill in the CCA part on that chart. More on that later.

>> *"Other Expenses"* This is used for anything you can't find a place for in the above categories. *Only use sparingly.* Ideally, there should be nothing here if you have done a good job finding places for all your expenses. Actually if you put a lot here, the taxman will scrutinize you much more closely.

One exception you could justify is "Professional Development" (professional courses, seminars, books, CD's) as mentioned above. Professional courses relevant to your career as an artist in any field qualify for this.

>> *"**Total Income**"* will automatically fill in for you by the tax software. Also your "Business Use of Home" total will appear if you had a positive income (not a loss). More on this later.

>> ***Partnerships**_:* There are two sections about Partnerships. This is only relevant for a formal legal Partnership. If you are a sole proprietor (a one person business), then you can ignore these bits. (A legal partnership is rare for artists, although possibly makes sense for an artist couple who work together.)

>> ***Home Studio, Vehicle, and Capital Assets (Equipment).*** The "Business Use of Home", Vehicle Claims and the "Capital Cost Allowance" will all be done as *yearend expense*, not ongoing through the year. You should keep all statements and receipts for these in a separate envelope so you can find them easily when you do your yearend tasks.

>> *"**Business Use of Home**" Expenses:* Here is where you can claim the portion of your home that you use for your art business. In order to claim that space, it *must* be *only* for your art-related

business, such as a visual art studio, office, music room, dance / performance studio/space.So a dining room table, living room sofa, kitchen table, corner of a bedroom, rec room which is also used for weight lifting *does not count.*

The room must be *only* for an art studio or computer room/office or art storage. Or at least a portion which is physically separated by a permanent room divider or curtain.

In order to calculate what percentage of the total home applies to your business use of home, you will need to do some measuring. Once done correctly , you will use the same percentage every year (unless you add or subtract from the space for some reason).

Follow these steps:

1.   Measure the space you use as a studio and/or office and/or storage space for art. Include any hall area that is essentially part of that space.

2. Now calculate the overall square footage for the total home. (The form allows either metric or

British measure. But be consistent throughout both accounting and tax records.)

Only count the garage if you use it *entirely* for art storage or other art use. Using the garage occasionally for a home art show would not count unless used that way quite frequently. Advice from an accountant could be useful on that point.

If you have a fairly new home you may have builder's plans which would show the measurements for each room.

Otherwise, or if you have changed or added anything, measure all the rooms, including baths, and halls.

Ignore the garage if it is used for general storage and/or your vehicles and ignore unfinished parts of the home (furnace room, cold storage, etc.) to get the total area of the house or apartment/condo.

3. *Divide the small number by the large number.* The result is the percentage for your studio/office. If per chance the number is above 25%, I recommend to *reduce* it to no more than 25%, and then jig the numbers to fit.

This is nothing to do with taxes, but it could affect your zoning and get you in trouble with your city by-laws. Most cities have a space limit for having a home business, and it is usually 25% with no formalities. The only exception would be if you are zoned commercial or live far out in the country.

If you are zoned residential, and claim over that 25%, the difference would be subject to capital gains tax on sale of the property.In Canada your principal residence is exempt from capital gains tax, so preserving this tax advantage is a good idea.

Inquire from your city about this. It is OK to inquire anonymously. Better safe than sorry.

4.On the tax form, you put the square footage of work space on the first line , and the total square footage of the house, on the second line . The software will calculate for you the right amount.

Do NOT use the "rooms" option. It is easy but usually very inaccurate because rooms are rarely all the same size, throwing off all your numbers.

All the amounts on the 'Business Use of Home' form are the totals for the house/ condo/ apartment. The software then does the percentage and puts your business percentage total on the form for you.

If you have a negative income on the first page of the T2125, then the software will NOT allow you to claim any Business Use of Home for that year. But never fear, you have not "lost" it.

The unused "Business Use of Home" carries forward to the next year, and on from that if necessary.

This is like money in the bank (no interest paid , however), and some year when you make the big bucks, that banked amount from all those negative years will get claimed automatically for you. Think of it as your savings account!

Canadian tax law says you may not increase a business loss with "Business Use of Home". You can only reduce a net income to zero with it (while still carrying forward any amount not used).

In case you forget that, the tax software will remember that for you. You do not need to do any calculations about that yourself. We are just explaining so you understand what is happening.

As you can see in this form, the things you can claim are: *heat* (gas, coal, propane, whatever); *electricity*, general home *insurance* (not your art insurance), general *maintenance and repairs* if any, *mortgage interest* (look on your last statement of the year, they will have that amount on the bottom), *property taxes*, and "Other" where you would put *water/sewer, and water heater rental.*

Internet could also go under "Other" if you use it *extensively* for your business (online galleries, stock photo sales, your arts related websites, etc.) In recent years the Tax Department has added a section on the first page where you list any websites or companies through which you earn money re your art/business online, with the percentage of your overall gross income. If you claim a percentage of Internet costs here, be prepared to defend the logic if audited. This should be easier now than it used to be.

In that case you are claiming the same percentage as for the rest of Business Use of Home, as long as the percentage of your income from Internet is at or *above* the Business Use of Home percentage that particular year.

So some years you may be claiming business use of internet and other years not, depending on how much of you gross income is from Internet that particular year.

Keep in mind however that websites simply for self-promotion, but not used for generating sales, will not qualify for the Internet claim.

There is a line that says "*capital cost allowance (business part only)*". Do NOT claim this. If you do, and then sell your home, you would be liable for capital gains tax on that part of your home! Again, there is no federal tax on your principal residence in Canada. This may be different in other countries. Be sure to check on this.

Just because you can do something does not necessarily mean that you should do it. This is one example of that.

>>*Details of Equity:*

"*Details of*" section is sort of optional, as it has no real bearing on the totals or tax: total business liabilities, drawings for the year, and capital contributions for the year. This gives the taxman a general idea of whether your business is generally viable or not and could be useful FYI.

Liabilities are your debts at yearend (line of credit, credit card debt, etc.)

Drawings are total $$ withdrawn from the business assets for personal use.

Capital contributions are total money contributed into the business: capital from elsewhere (pension, salary, savings).

This info could be requested later if not filled in so it is good to keep track of it. It is useful to you in analyzing your business in any case. For instance, if you need to add a lot of money from personal sources to keep afloat, that could be a danger signal. And of course high liabilities could indicate trouble.

>> *Motor Vehicle Expenses*. You would claim this even if you are not claiming CCA (capital cost allowance) on the vehicle. On the Vehicle form, there is room for two vehicles. If one vehicle is personal and one is business, be sure to only claim the business vehicle portion of expenses. USA

please note, in Canada we use kilometers, while you use mileage .

The only way you can do the simpler percentage system based on x cents per kilometer is if you are incorporated. There is nothing in the unincorporated software to accommodate this method, although some accountants will claim there is.

So if you are unincorporated, you will enter the *kilometers you drove for **business** in the year* (you need to keep track of this over the year).

The easiest way to keep track is write on a calendar where you went as you go along, and number of kilometers, then add it up for the year. Or keep a log book or diary, if you are the organized type.

The software will divide this total by *the total km/mileage you drove for the year.* This will give you your business percentage for the year. This will vary year to year as your travel varies year to year.

What if you have not been keeping track?? If you did not record the starting mileage for this year, look at whatever maintenance records you have that are yearend last year or near beginning of this year and estimate that number.

The software will calculate the percentage that you will be allowed. It is recommended to tinker a bit to end up with a whole number for the percentage. (To be on the safe side, tinker down not up)

If you did not keep track of your mileage for last year, estimate based on known errands with receipts, known meetings, etc. and do better from now on. You live, you learn.

You can claim *fuel, and oil; interest,* if buying the auto on credit (see chart B*); insurance; license and registration; maintenance and repairs; leasing* if applicable (Chart C*); parking fees,* and any supplemental *business insurance* (unlikely for you).

As mentioned before, you enter the full amounts for the year and the tax software calculates the total for you based on your business use percentage. This is the same method as for "Business Use of Home".

It is unwise to claim over 50% as Business Use for your vehicle as it might be hard to justify and may be challenged.

For visual artists: Things that would be justifiable: going to art events and meetings, getting art supplies, trips by auto that are directly related to your art (such as you are showing at an art fair in another city), trips to do art/photography for your artistic output (and which you can prove), etc.

For *musicians/performers*: going to concerts/events to learn what other related musicians are doing (within reason: be prepared to justify). Or travel to your own local event in which you are performing, travelling in your own vehicle (wherein you are expected to cover your own travel cost).

For writers: travel related to whatever you are writing about locally or must travel on assignment to or on spec in hopes of getting your work published (especially when it does later get published).

For musicians/actors: mileage related to music performances/playing on tour wherein you need to drive your own vehicle.

Examples of when you could claim over 50%: you took a long trip by vehicle to various of your art shows across country. Or a trip to photograph a large part of the country for a coffee table book or to do research for your art. Or for musicians and performers, a long music tour or performance tour where you have to cover your own travel.

As with the Business Use Of Home, use a round number, so you don't end up with awkward fractions . More on this in Audit section.

>> *Calculation of Capital Cost Allowance (CCA):*

The total claimed will magically appear on your front page of expenses. (Any specific terminology referred to here are related to Canadian law. Other countries will be similar but may possibly use different terminology.)

This is where you enter all items that cost over $200, that you claim gradually over time. (Other countries may have a different limit.)These are called *capital expenditures for fixed assets.*

This means that these are major expensive items that will last a long time, and that you claim over the years as they depreciate in value. That is why it is an "allowance" which applies to your larger capital costs. The % claimed is the amount set by the tax department for your tax software.

It is actually *optional to claim CCA*. If it would increase your net loss, then it is legal but may not be advisable to claim. In order to not claim, change the % column to zero for any Class you don't want to claim. More on that in the Audit section.

General: *the 50% rule*: This is applied to all new purchases. The software works this out automatically for you, but it is good to understand it: The first year of a CCA purchase, you can only claim 50% of the amount you would otherwise claim. That is because you might have purchased at the beginning or end of the year or anywhere in between, so 50% is an average. The next year and thereafter, you may claim the full amount you are allowed. Again the software keeps track and does all that for you automatically.

On the CCA form you will see the first column is which *Class* (8,10, 45, etc.).

Next is the **UCC** (*Undepreciated Capital Cost)* that you start with at the beginning of the year, left over from the previous year.

Then *Cost of Additions* in the year (the detail of that goes in Area B and auto inserts from there).

Then *Proceeds of Disposition,* meaning you sold something second hand and got something for it. Details go in Area D, and they will auto-insert.

All classes except motor vehicles go together.

Actually you only fill in the Additions (what you bought in the taxation year) and Dispositions (second hand sales). The software works out everything else and pops it into the right places.

There are many **Classes of assets** but only a few Classes that would apply to artists so we will only deal with those:

Class 10 is for old computers bought before March 23, 2004, claimed at 30%. (Some accountants use this for new computers as well, but that is not correct.)

The newer classes you would use are ***Class 12*** for *software* at 100% (it takes 2 years to write off, however, due to the 50% rule).

Class 45 (at 45%), *50* (at 55%), *52* (at 100%) are for *newer computers* and systems software (Mac, Windows) , also peripherals that physically connect to the computer like printers and scanners. Which one you will use will depend on when the computer or peripheral was bought. See your tax software for dates and details.

These Classes can change from year to year, so be sure to see your software (under Help, CCA Classes) to be sure you have it right for you. The exact date you purchased is what makes the difference as to how much is claimed.

Class 8 is for anything that doesn't fit into the other classes. Like furniture, cameras, studio equipment, expensive tools, etc. at 20%, This is used a lot by photo-based artists and sculptors.

Your motor vehicle is **Class 10.1** or **10** depending on the description, both at 30%.

The last column is *UCC (Undepreciated Capital Cost)* at end of year and is the amount that carries forward to the next year. Remember that the percentage claim is based on the UCC remaining from the year before, *not* the percentage of the amount paid, so it can take many years to write anything off.

Very important: Please note that you can only claim for *all* the items in the class or *none* of that class, and *only at the set percentage* if claiming.

Terminal loss can only be done at the end of the business (retirement or the business is dissolved prior to incorporation) or your death or when there is *absolutely* no physical thing that is functional in the particular Class.

The only class you might be able to do a terminal loss for, while still in business, is Class 10 when eventually nothing is left in it (that is, your very old computers have all been disposed of, or are non-functional). And possibly Class 12 if nothing in it.

The details for how to do this is in the help section of your software. Terminal losses will also help to reduce tax on the estate before assets (mostly the visual art) are passed to the beneficiary.

Building Dispositions (meaning sale of a building) You likely won't deal with building dispositions, unless it is a separate studio building which has been sold..

Other Dispositions, means that you have sold an item in a Class (second hand), and report what you received for it. The software will do the calculation for you to remove that amount from that Class.

>>*Yearend Tasks for Accounting*:

These accounting tasks are done in your accounting software at yearend or whenever you do your taxes. Remember for accounting software, you are using double entry method. See Part I for details.

1.Compile your **Business Use Of Home** statements, receipts, and add up the totals for each category. Make accounts in your accounting program for each category, such as "electricity" or "hydro". Use a "cash" account for the category part of your double entry system. (See Part I for details.)

Remember since you have already paid these amounts for the household, this is a paper-only transaction to facilitate your business accounting claim. This is why you use the "cash, yearend adjustment" method (from Owners Capital) so that the amount won't show up as a new purchase. Remember you already paid the heating, water, etc., so you can't claim you paid the business portion over again. Therefore you will need to "deposit" enough cash from Owners Capital to cash account as "to cash to cover yearend" for yearend adjustments.

For the expense category, use "*__Business Use of Home Expense__*" or "*__Car and Truck Expense__*" so the software knows this is a yearend adjustment and not a "real" expense like your supplies, etc. Then "draw" from your paper "cash" for each paper transaction.

Get a bookkeeper or accountant to check that you have this right the first time you do it, to be on the safe side.

Example: Let's say your claim is 20% of the house for studio. You would add up your hydro bills, and take 20% of that and claim that amount into your Hydro account in your accounting software, and out of paper "cash". Remember, in your accounting software you are using the paper "cash" (which is just for the convenience of making your calculations for the taxes).

But on the tax software, remember you put the full amount for the year, and the software calculates the percentage for you. *Two different methods.*

It is best to do the tax software amount first as the tax software may end up with a few pennies +/- due to the tax software doing the math a bit more exactly. I do each category one by one in the tax software just to check, then adjust the accounting end to match if necessary. Sometimes your calculation of % may be ,say, 30% while the tax software may say 29.9% . So go with the tax software total as that is same as tax department uses.

2. For **vehicle(s),** again use paper "cash" for the paper claim in your accounting software, and set up accounts for each category under "Vehicle". Total the expenses you are claiming, and enter the percentage into those accounts (example: Suppose your percentage to claim for vehicle is 30%: gas total @ 30 % = amount to claim for gas).

Again remember that for the tax software you are entering the full amount and the software is calculating the % for you automatically. Do the one by one as for Business use of Home above and then adjust the accounting claim accordingly.

3. *For your CCA* if you choose to claim it: you may claim one Class and not another. To get the biggest bang for your buck, claim Software (Class 12 in Canada) first, then claim the better classes of computers, as the claims are higher. You may NOT change the percentage from, say, 30% to 10%. You must claim *all of a class* at the full rate or not at all. Again use the paper "cash" method to record, and the expense goes in "*Depreciation Expense*".

Accrual amounts: (Only farmers and fishermen are on the cash method) Accrual method means that even if a sale occurred in December but you did not get paid till January or later, you have to pay tax on the sale for the tax year in which the sale occurred.

 Just remember not to pay the tax again for the year in which you did finally get paid! Keep careful records of anything that could be accrued.

Also you can also "accrue" an expense by claiming it in the year actually used rather than the year paid.

Again keep 2 copies of the receipt, one for year expense is incurred, and one for year claimed.

Sales Tax:

To Register or Not:

NOTE: IF YOU LIVE OUTSIDE OF CANADA, there may be similar situations concerning your sales taxes (state taxes for USA, VAT tax for UK, etc.)

Another note, the *QST* is only in the province of Quebec, and is the equivalent of the HST elsewhere in Canada.

Many artists avoid registering for HST/GST/QST, assuming it is a lot of trouble and work. Actually it is automated by your accounting software, and only takes a few minutes a year to file.

You can choose to file as often as monthly (for a very busy business) to quarterly, semi-annually to annually. Whatever works for you.

Filing is best done at tax time, although the deadline is actually June 15 for HST (Canada) if you do not owe tax. But it is April 30, if you owe sales tax..

And of course the big advantage is that you get all your sales tax back on your business purchases. This includes all sales tax on large purchases such as computers, cameras, etc. which would have to be amortized (CCA).

If you spend more sales tax than you charge, you get a lovely refund. If automated via NETFILE, you can arrange to have it autopay directly into your business related bank account.

In Canada, you are **required to register for HST/GST/QST** as soon as you *gross* **$30,000** in *any 12 month period.* That means revenue only, not revenue less expenses. It also includes all gross self-employed revenue which you would claim on your T2125, including contract teaching and any other contract work where you are not on salary with benefits deducted from your pay cheque. The trigger point could happen at any time during a calendar year. Watch your revenue receipts. Keep a tally as you go along.

Once registered, you can't switch back and forth from one year to another. Once in, you are in for life unless you "retire".

Also, since it is *any 12 month period*, that could go from, say, October to September, so you could find that a big income at the end of the previous tax year could combine with income in the first part of the current tax year to bump you into obligatory Sales Tax territory *at any time*. If you had considerable income near the end of one year, be sure to keep a close eye on your gross income the next year.

Remember the Tax Department can charge interest and penalties starting as soon as you should have been charging Sales Tax, *retroactively*, once they determine that that is the case.

Once registered, *you must* charge GST/PST/HST/ QST on your artwork, and other art related services which are taxable.

 But you can also claim the tax back (GST or HST or QST) on **all** *of your purchases that you claim for your business* and this can be a *substantial refund* if you are in the red or have a low taxable income. It will also reduce your taxes on net income.

Also you can register at any time *before you are required to,* to take advantage of any refunds as you go along. But once in, you are in, don't opt out. The Taxman will be watching you very carefully if you try to opt out. (It's legal, NOT a good idea.)

Decide if registering for sales tax would be useful for you. This is most useful for photo-based artists and sculptors, due to the high costs of their media. It is also useful for musicians, performers, and writers who travel a lot at their own expense.

When given the choice of whether to register or not due to low income, some visual artists prefer not to register in the belief that the lower price for the visual art will pull in more sales. Maybe,.. maybe not… Many registered artists include the sales tax in the price of their art to be competitive, negating any apparent sales advantage to non-registered artists!

Also there is the possibility that the buying public may assume a lower level of professionalism if sales tax is not charged, that is, they may make the assumption that the visual artist is a hobbyist instead of a professional. This assumption may or may not be correct depending on who is selling.

(That said, it is normal for registered visual artists to include the tax at an Art Expo featuring individual artists as opposed to art galleries.)

Out of Province Sales:

If you make an *out-of-province sale in Canada*, and you are registered, you would charge whatever the HST is or GST for the province *to which* you are selling If the province you are selling to charges PST, you would not charge the PST however.

The list of taxes in all the provinces is on the CRA (Canada Revenue Agency) website and this is kept up to date.

Here is the summary:

QST:14.975%; HST ON/NL/NB 13%; HST in PEI 14%; HST in NS 15%; and GST at 5% in AL.

All other provinces, territories are on GST/PST (GST is at 5% for all of them). By the way, BC has reverted back to the PST/GST method from HST.

Note that your *QuickBooks®* will only calculate HST re your own province (and any other that is the same, plus GST only, and tax exempt/ zero tax).

So to do business with any other province with a different HST rate you will need to adjust via an "adjustment" on your invoice, then manually make the correction when you file on the CRA website. Filing can be manually done online with amounts typed in , so this is possible, not a problem.

Also, if registered, you are claiming the amount *without* tax as the expense amount. If you are *not* registered, you are claiming the expense *including the tax.*

This means, in practice that you can claim more items in full (not amortized via CCA) if you are registered. See detail in CCA section above...

In summary, if you are NOT registered, you do NOT charge HST/GST/PST but you also may NOT claim any sales tax back. However you would charge PST (in any province that is still on that system) regardless of your gross income.

Some provinces are currently still on PST/GST as of now but be aware that they may be changing to HST at some point in time. Watch the news about this. That sort of thing is always well publicized in the press.

For those registered, remember that some sources of taxable income, like visual art galleries, stock photo agencies, performance venues, etc. may charge sales tax *directly to the purchaser and remit it*. For those sources, you do not charge sales tax again as they have already done it for you.

NETFILING for HST/GST/QST is done manually online. That is, you fill in the amounts yourself. You do not have to file at same time as general tax if you are expecting a refund. But of you owe tax , of course you would file by the same deadline as for general income tax, to avoid any interest and penalties.

Donations of Art

IS IT ADVANTAGEOUS TAX-WISE TO DONATE your visual art works to charities in Canada? Not really, when you look at the money. Yes, you can claim the charitable deduction on the personal side, *however you must claim the same amount as "income" (a "deemed disposition") on the business side* even though you did not receive any money! In effect, one cancels the other out.

In addition you may have to pay out of pocket to *ship* the art to the charity. Also, the deemed income could trigger *quarterly payments* ongoing!

If the donation is to an institution that is *not* a registered charity, you would have deemed "income" to claim on paper, but no deduction, which would result in net tax to you even though you did not receive any money!

In addition, to donate to some charities, especially universities, you may have to jump through as many hoops as you would to apply for a grant. But don't just assume that they will want to have your work! They may require an application process, a jurying, and could decline your work even if it is top quality. There may be many complex criteria, which could change over time, bureaucratic "little boxes", which can vary widely from charity to charity. Proceed carefully. If you apply and are told you have been declined, ask why, so you will know where you stand in general and re other possibilities. You may be surprised at the answers.

Here is the procedure, should you want to do it:

This is called the *2-step process*, and according to accountants is becoming the norm today.

You invoice the charity for the work. They issue you a payment. You donate the *exact same amount* back to the charity. They issue you a charitable receipt. You have a "real" sale, plus a donation.

Of course the charity needs to trust you enough to wait for the donation back. They may require you to sign an agreement that you will follow through with the donation part to offset the payment.

The *"traditional" process* of donating the visual art and receiving a Charitable Donation-in-Kind receipt now requires a *professional appraisal* in writing, and you enter the name and address of the Appraiser on the Tax form. This can be challenged by the taxman. You may also be expected to cover the cost of the appraisal yourself. In the past, one did not have to do the appraisal part, so the cost of appraisal was moot.

There may be, on the other hand, some non-monetary advantage to you for donating your visual art. You may feel the record of a theoretical "sale" would have some professional advantage for you, from the point of the fact that your work is now at a prestigious museum, gallery or institution.

Also, there may be the consideration that your art would be, hopefully, well housed and cared for after your passing, and would save tax on the estate, which could be some comfort.

That said, in Canada, there is the situation wherein the visual artist's work is accepted by an *accredited* museum or gallery under the Canadian Cultural Property Review Board (CCPRB). There is a huge rigmarole to do this. However, then you do not have to claim the "income", which is a tax advantage, while you can still claim the donation credit.

In order to get this set up, your work needs to be "defended" as *culturally important* to the institution and /or the nation. They actually use the term "national treasure"! In other words, this is for mid-career and senior career Canadian visual artists who have gained a notable measure of fame, not emerging or early career artists.

 Ask your accountant re details as there may be advantages and disadvantages to this route. If unsure, they may refer you on to a copyright lawyer for further advice.

There may be equivalent systems in other countries. Generally the USA has been ahead of Canada in many areas like this for many years. And the same may apply to other countries as well.

For *gifts of art to non-charities and individuals* there is also deemed disposition at normal value and sales tax is applied (or not) as normal for you.

To NETFILE

or Not:

"NETFILE" IS A SYSTEM THAT ENABLES YOU to file your taxes online. This system may have other names in other countries. It saves a lot of printing out of the forms. And of course beats the heck out of doing tax forms by hand (I shudder to remember those !!).

However you are expected to keep all your bank statements and investment forms for your records in case they ask for them later, which could be any time in the next 7 years. See Audit section for more on this.

Contrary to popular myth, Internet filing does *not* trigger more audits. Actually the Tax Department loves it because it saves them a lot of time manually inputting all those numbers.

Also there is less chance of error due to inadvertent incorrect input of your manual numbers, such as a misplaced decimal point. So NETFILE is recommended..

Caution: Just be sure everything is *perfect* before you do the NETFILE, as it can take up to 3 months to correct an error ! (They deal with urgent matters before corrections.)

Both *QuickBooks®* and *Turbo Tax®* will print out very nice reports that will be all you could ever need. The Taxman loves those nice neat reports. Doing anything by hand these days is so fraught with likelihood of errors, that it just sets the teeth on edge. *Not recommended!* A bookkeeper can help with data input if you can't cope with that, but it is so easy nowadays, I am sure you can learn.

Nitty Gritty Summary:

What have you learned so far?

1. There are many expenses that you as an artist can and should claim.

2. You now know what exactly to claim and how and where.

3. There are pros and cons re registering for Sales taxes

4. Donating your art may or may not be appropriate for you.

5. Filing via the internet is fast , easy and can be an advantage for you

MY NOTES

_____

_____

_____

_____

_____

_____

_____

_____

_____

_____

_____

_____

_____

_____

_____

<u>MORE NOTES</u>

_____

_____

_____

_____

_____

_____

_____

_____

_____

_____

_____

_____

_____

_____

_____

_____

Part III

What If You Are Audited?

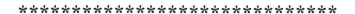

****

Part III

What If You
Are Audited?

**Demystifying the Audit:
Your Rights, The Procedures,
How To Win Your Audit**

My personal experience:

Of course the very thought of being audited can send chills down your spine. It surely scared me a few years ago. But knowing your rights and the legal process takes a lot of the stress and fear away. That is why this section of the book was created, to help you on that.

Much of the detail here is based on personal experience, salted with experience from my financial planner years, plus the adventures of students who attended my seminars.

Most of what was denied was contested in my Appeal, (self-written, with the kind guidance of my accountant), and the results were very successful. Hopefully, my experience will help you if you ever need that help.

Use of an accountant is referred to here and there throughout as an integral part of the Audit process, so there is not a separate section for that.

Why You Are Being Audited:

(what triggers an audit)

THERE ARE MANY POSSIBLE REASONS why you might be audited, or sadly no reason at all (just the luck of the draw) .The following is per Canadian law. Other countries may be more strict or less strict. Here is where some personal advice from your accountant could be pertinent if unsure how to proceed on certain things.

Here are some reasons you could get audited and/or challenged during an audit:

A. Inconsistent filing, or lack of filing

B. Some expenses are deemed too high

C. Non-allowable expenses have been claimed

D. Some receipts are not acceptable

E. You have been negative for quite some time

F. Inconsistent claims

G. It's time…

H. Your number came up…

>A. Inconsistent Filing or Lack of Filing.

You have been in business as an artist for several years but have *never filed your expenses before, or have been filing off and on.*

*It does not matter whether you are in the red or in the black. You are expected to always file your income and expenses **every year.***

It is very important to be very consistent about this. The taxman tends to be suspicious of inconsistent filing. They may assume that you are hiding something in the years you did not file.

If you did not keep good records in the non-filed years, you may be in a position of trying to prove something that does not exist, especially if you did not keep your receipts.

If you have not been filing due to ongoing losses, you can back file yourself, but expect several months before you get any refunds you would have missed out on as they have to go back to all the previous tax forms. Receipts are needed for every expense claimed, of course.

So, if you have been in business for years, but have not filed at all, or inconsistently, you should *get to an accountant pronto* and see what you can do. Accountants can apply for amnesty for you for up to 3 years if you owe tax and if you own up voluntarily before the audit ax falls. *Only an accountant can do this amnesty* for you as there are special forms that only the accountant will have.. This is one case where you really can't DIY !

The accountant can be either a CGA or CA, it doesn't matter which.

>B. Some expenses deemed too high.

This is a very common situation. For artists, there are some danger areas: travel, car and Business Use of Home.

1. Travel:

This is the biggest area for over-claiming:

For instance, an artist and her family of 4 takes a vacation to Florida for, let's say,10 days. They have fun and relaxation for 9 days, and she does some sketches, photos for one day or equivalent. She claims the entire trip for her whole family as a business expense. No–no! This is *not reasonable*.

(The term *"reasonable in the circumstances"* comes up a lot with the Tax Department.)

Since, in that example, she only did "business related activities" for 1 day out of 10, she should only claim 10% of only *her* portion of the airfare, or mileage if she drove down, or car rental, and 10% of her accommodation and meals.

Let's say the airfare was $2000 for the 4 of them, and her part was $500. She would, in this example, claim $50 (10% of her portion) for the airfare. For meals, she should only claim 50% of one day's worth of meals for herself only. (Remember, meals are at 50% as you have to eat any way. And you don't claim the tip if it is in cash as theoretically the tip is "optional".)

As you can see, the travel issue is complex and needs to be dealt with carefully. If in doubt, err on the side of caution. And/or get advice.

The only way you would claim for family would be if the cost is the same for "single" as for "double" or "family" rate, as for some accommodation. Or if the family is needed for the trip (such as used as models for visual art related images, or a partner is helping on an art expo booth, or co-performers in a concert as back-up where you are covering their expenses, or testing out recipes for your articles as a travel writer, etc.).

Accommodation which is very luxurious could be

challenged as unnecessary. You are expected to live modestly, not high off the hog. Also very expensive dining out could be challenged. This is not to say that you must rent run down, shabby, places in bad parts of town. Or eat at greasy spoons. But middle class accommodation and meals are considered "normal" and "reasonable".

Meals at the usual government rates are deemed OK. Groceries for making your own meals where you rent a condo or apartment for the trip , are claimable as long as they are reasonable (for instance, lobster and caviar would not be considered "normal' grocery items.) Alcoholic drinks are usually not claimed as they are "not necessary" and/or "not reasonable".

By the way, you may *not* claim trip cancelation *insurance or travel health insurance*, or extra life insurance for air travel. You are expected to live dangerously: extra insurance is considered an optional perk! No kidding!!

It is commonly thought that some people joke that as long as you do some little thing that is business, you can claim a whole trip, but that is *not* the case. Be very careful about this category of expense as they tend to watch it *very* closely. *Better to under claim, than over-claim..*

For *local trips* in your province or nearby, where you travel in your vehicle, only claim the part of mileage that pertains to the business portion. If part is personal, and part is business, 50% or less would be business mileage.

If most is personal (home for Christmas, but you went out and did some lovely photos of the snow one afternoon, which will later be used as the basis for paintings, or you performed at a home town event for which you were paid.) then you would only claim the local driving that specifically applies to your art.

Remember the key is to only claim what you could defend as *"reasonable in the circumstances"*.

2. *The Vehicle*:

It is wise to keep your percentage of the vehicle(s) to a total of no more than 50% of all your driving, even if it should be higher. It is hard to justify more than 50%, unless you are in a position where you are required to travel extensively for you art, and you can prove that. Be prepared to plead your case and keep a log book of the mileage.

For instance, travelling extensively to work on a photo book, or series of lectures, music tour/performances in a wide geographic area, or visual art shows in far flung places, or a travelling exhibition would be good examples of where you may be able to go over the 50% for the vehicle, assuming you or your partner is driving.

3. *Business Use of Home*:
Claiming over 25% of your home has implications re city by- laws re zoning, and could trigger capital gains tax on sale of the home.

For the taxman, there is no problem re the 25% but it is not wise to go over 35% even if you zoning might allow it. (such as, where you are in a commercial zone or way out in the country.) Check with your municipality about this. It is OK to find out anonymously. This is one case where a bit of tinkering may be necessary to keep both levels of government in sync.

4. *A Very Large Item is claimed:*

Something is claimed in full that the taxman would see as odd, and very expensive may not pass the sniff test and could ring bells. It depends on what it is. It may be something that is not obviously part of your art related expenses, or may be related to other self-employed income making ventures, in an effort to support your art expenses.

Quite often, this can be defended, depending on whether it is *"reasonable in the circumstances"*. It may be useful to get an accountant to help with the language here, if challenged.

>C. *Non allowable expenses are claimed.*

Look back *to   Nitty Gritty (Part II)* for what you can claim. Some strange expenses claims have come to light:

Example 1: A whole case of champagne for a private art selling event in the artist's home. A smaller amount would likely be accepted, but a whole case might be a bit extreme as it might not be seen as *"essential"* or *"reasonable"* (depending on the details re venue, sales total , type of clientele).

Example 2: Special wardrobe and makeup for a performance art event. This could be defended, depending on details and exact language used. Accountant guidance re language useful here. For instance: "theatrical costume" in lieu of "clothes", and "theatrical make up" or "theatrical paint" may work better than just "makeup".

As an aside: One category that is usually challenged, as mentioned in Part II is *home telephone, your cell phone, and internet service.*

One would think that the *phones* would go under "telephone and utilities", and that internet could go under "office expenses". But that "telephone and utilities" line is for phones and hydro for *rented* studio spaces, that is, business- rated extra service, and for phones that are under a business name separate from the family phones. Unless this kind of service is essential for your business, it is not financially viable as the rates are somewhat higher than family rates, which offsets any tax claim advantage.

It seems that the reality is, so far (and this could change), that the taxman considers home related phones to be entirely personal. Yet today many artists use their smart phones for much more than phone calls, such as photography, even some apps that could be business related. One can only hope that eventually this modern usage will be recognized as legitimate business in future!

Long distance charges for both landlines and cell that can be logged via statements, and verified as definitely "business" may be claimed, however . Be sure to keep the appropriate cell or phone statements. These could go under "office expense".

The telephone/cell issue is a topic you may want to discuss with your accountant. Probably opinions differ on this point. It could be worth the fight if most of the rest that is disallowed is unfounded, while you could concede on some other points.

If you use *the internet* extensively and could argue that it is an essential tool for your art business, , you should be able to claim it. The appropriate place would be in Business Use of Home under "Other", at same rate as all the "other" expenses there like water/sewer. That is, at 25% or less. This is one category that has changed in the past few years, in recognition of the many internet based businesses today. This will be especially pertinent for artists selling their art or services online on their own websites or with online galleries or professional websites. Progress...

Concerning **inappropriate items**: You may come across items that you thought at the time would be claimable expenses for your business, but later decided they did not work, or were not useful for your business after all. So you decided that you did not want to claim them.

These would be better described as "personal item" or "personal various" and recorded as into "Drawings" not into an expense category. That way they do not show up under expenses, and will not cause issues later.

Remember you can make such corrections at any time and the accounting software will make all updates needed for you. Do these adjustments *before* you do the tax returns to avoid future issues.

>D. *Receipts not acceptable*

The Tax Department will not accept expenses that are not properly proven. There must be an *acceptable receipt for all expenses.* They will, for instance, not accept *cancelled cheques/checks* as receipts. If paying by cheque/check, you must also get a written receipt of some kind, with the item, amount, date, who you purchased from or paid for a service, and preferably the address of the vendor if possible.

The other thing not accepted is those tissue *credit card receipts* (the ones you get when the old fashioned click machine is used.) In addition to that receipt you would then also need a written receipt like the one described above.

When you get the double receipt, like you some-times get for the *thermals,* the one you need is the one that itemizes the goods purchased. The short one with the credit card info is not needed for the audit. The thermals that will fade away to white will need to be scanned or photocopied while still readable. See **The Audit Process** for what to do with those thermals .

>E. ***You have been negative*** for some time, and there is concern that perhaps you are not a viable business.

For visual artists, a field audit (visit to your art studio or visual art show) could reveal to the taxman that you prices are so low that even if you sold a large portion of your annual output, you still would not be able cover all your art production expenses at break even. In that case, all your expenses could be disallowed and you could officially be designated as a "hobbyist" and no longer permitted to claim any art related expenses. You would however still be expected to pay tax on any sales, claimed under "other income", as is the norm for hobbyists.

You need to have a ***"reasonable expectation of profit"*** in order to be allowed to continue to claim expenses as a professional artist. Do a little math: see if you would have to sell *more* than 60% of your annual art output in order to break even on your art related expenses (*without* counting any income from art or any other sources and including worst case scenario commission). If so, you would need to make more art…

Include in your calculation your studio rental or Business Use of Home but do *not* include motor vehicle or CCA expense.

To do this, take the average of 3 years of expenses not including CCA, and divide that by the average price (adjusted for your usual gallery commission) . That will give you the total number of works you would need to sell to break even!

Similar calculations could be appropriate for writers, musicians, performers. If you need help with this to justify your professional standing, get an accountant to help with the logic, and appropriate arguments in your case.

Now don't panic if the news is bad re your ***reasonable expectation of profit***. Actually they don't expect you to make a profit annually on an ongoing basis. This is just a paper exercise to see whether there is a ***reasonable* expectation of profit on *paper***, which is a long way from assuming you will *actually* make a profit each year. The taxman is well used to artists being chronically in the red. And they well know that as long as you are following all the rules and can justify your expenses, that is fine. The taxman only needs to wait till you pass away, and their ship will come in in the end, from your estate. Sad but true.

In fact for every dollar you claim in expenses, the taxman will receive at least $2 in tax based on the deemed disposition of the estate. And that assumes zero inflation. Which of course we know is unlikely. So the real factor will be somewhat higher than 2! *So there is no need to feel guilty or embarrassed or shy about what you claim.* You are entitled to your claims (assuming you are following the tax rules), and much more will end up paid to the taxman from the estate in the long run...

See the Epilogue/Estate Planning section for more.

>F Inconsistent claims; You claim one way one year and another way another year: being consistent is very important. Once you get straightened out on how to do things, stick to one way to claim. Don't keep changing what categories you use for a particular expense, unless the tax law requires it (such as all meals used to be separate, now meals while travelling are under "travel".)

>G. It's time:

You have been audited before or this is your first audit: the *number of years since last audit* is 4 to 10 years (or maybe never, if all is well).

They assume it could take several years to start getting a positive net income so you don't need to worry the first few years. I have heard as low as 5 and as high as 20 for a first time audit. In other words, no one really knows, including accountants!

Or...

>H. Your 'Number' just came up !:

Unfortunately, sometimes you get audited for no apparent reason, like all artists in a geographic area, people whose name starts with S, or just no reason, pure chance: Or several small things over a period of years could build up a picture.

General note: It is always critical to be correct and honest in whatever you claim. If you try to "fudge" the truth or outright lie, you can bet on getting caught. The taxman watches carefully and tends to expect that behavior.

How to Avoid
Being Audited

DO IT RIGHT AS PER THE FIRST 2 PARTS OF THIS BOOK! And pay special attention to what triggers an audit. The biggest reason is *non-filing or inconsistent filing*. Be sure to file annually after this...

It is useful to take ongoing seminars on bookkeeping and tax law since by taking advantage of such topics you will pick up more pointers.

In spite of doing my own accounts for over 40 years, starting with pencil and ledger books the old fashioned way (having taken some accredited accounting courses), it is still a priority to grab any accounting related seminar to be found, just in case there is some gem not known that would be helpful to me. You never finish learning.

That said, however, you may find that "free" seminars are sometimes sales pitches for whatever accounting firm, and often the info is incomplete or more attuned to incorporated businesses than sole proprietors. Also they are usually aimed at the general public, not artists. A financial/bookkeeping seminar that is attuned to the needs of visual artists in particular is hard to find, with the exception of seminars run by CARFAC.

As an aside, if you are a visual artist, joining CARFAC is highly recommended if you are a professional . CARFAC has been a very valuable source of advice for me over the past 40+ years. It is well worth the modest fee (which is tax deductible under "Fees").

Your Legal Rights in the Audit Process

IN CANADA WE ARE FORTUNATE that there is a reasonable, rational, and fair process in place for audits. One hears of horror stories, but usually there are two sides to any story and sometimes it is not so much *what* is challenged by the artist but *how* it is challenged. More on that later.

1. *Sometimes the artist has tried DIY but should have gotten advice from an accountant.* If you follow the advice in this book, you should be well set to do it right, but if your situation is very complex or unusual, you are well advised to get a side of advice from your accountant.

2. *You have the right to* **Rebuttal** *to the first challenge of your submission, and also an* **Appeal** *process after that.* If done appropriately, the results should be fair and equitable to you in your situation. They will tell you about the rebuttal process, but the taxman may *not* necessarily tell you about the Appeal process.

You will find out about the **Appeal** by consulting an accountant , and this often makes all the difference in the world.

If the Appeal process had been known to me in the beginning, it would have saved me a lot of worry, stress and time. And if the accountant had been brought into it at the Rebuttal stage, that could have saved months of work.

3. You also have the right to *use Access to Information* if needed. More on this later.

The Audit Process

1. IF/WHEN YOU GET THAT DREADED LETTER in the mail, that you are being audited, you will be given *30 days to file your paperwork*, with clear instructions on what they want to see..

If it is December, and you have the 30 days to file, ask for 60 days. They will usually give you that as they will be on leave over Christmas anyway, so that would be considered reasonable.

It is not uncommon to get *The Letter* in late November or early December, and related to the latest tax year filed, or even a previous year.

2. Technically the taxman can audit back a far as 7 years. So it is required to keep all your paperwork back 7 years, including the current taxation year.

You should *always keep records* of the purchase of all fixed assets (the ones you claim over time as CCA), and all in one envelope, so you can find them easily.

While you should keep all your ledgers, software files and print outs indefinitely, receipts for consumables that are claimed in full can bite the dust after 7 years.

It is also good to print out all your journals, ledgers, tax returns, and keep them in binders, one binder per taxation year. This is great for quick reference.

3.   You will be required to *provide all your ledgers of expenses* (but not the bank, cash, credit cards) together with all the receipts that are on those ledgers. A ledger is a list of all expenses in a category, like Supplies or Office Expenses, etc. Your software will have a way to print those out. These ledgers are also a great way to get a handle on what you have spent on what.

4. A Caution: Those thermal receipts that many big box stores give nowadays will fade to white in a year to 2 years. *Remember that the tax dept. requires original receipts that are legible.* So ask for a paper receipt where possible. If that is not available, scan or photocopy your thermals while they are still readable, annually. Then use a ballpoint pen and on the thermal, trace over the name of the store, the main item, the total, tax and net total. That way you could provide *the original + the scan which is fully readable.* Certainly, it is a pain in the butt but that is the problem with the thermal receipts. Thank modern "progress"!

Scan them by category (gas, office supplies, etc.) as that is the way you would need them later, if ever audited. Or by month (remember you will need to separate out by category if you get audited.) Doing this little chore at once or twice a year is a good idea.

If you scan as opposed to photocopy, there is no need to print out until needed for the audit as you can save them with appropriate file names so they can be found later.

WHAT IF YOU ARE AUDITED?

Put your scanned receipts all together in a folder on your computer labelled in a way that makes sense to you.

Now, when preparing for your first submission of the requested receipts, you will need to scan (or photocopy) all your other receipts that you have not already scanned. This is because you have to send them   the *originals* for every single purchase, including your vehicle gas receipts (probably you had to scan those), so you will want to have copies in case the originals get lost in the mail or at the tax department.

You need to find all the original receipts that show on all the expense ledgers, including the thermals + scans as above, and arrange them in calendar order, staple them together, with each expense ledger, including Business Use of Home and vehicle.

This stage is the most time consuming part of the whole exercise.

5. The taxman will reply to your mailing of the receipts, usually several months later with a very long list of what they are contesting and disallowing and **a bill for what they claim you owe**.

It is important to pay whatever they charge you, as that will **stop the clock** *on the interest* they would otherwise charge.

The whole process from A to Z can take 12 months to 24 months, so you definitely don't want interest to be piling up all that time as it can greatly increase what you may have to ultimately be responsible for paying, and can also result in penalties, which can be substantial.

The tax interest rate is generally somewhat more than bank loan rates. So, even if you are sure you are 100% right and they are 100% wrong, pay up and go through the process, after which you will get back whatever they owe you.

6. *Prep for your* **Rebuttal***: Go over the list you receive very carefully.* This would be a good time to get an accountant to help understand what you are up against, and how much of it is founded in law and what is contestable. That is, what mistakes have you made, and what can you fight them about.

Don't just assume it is all OK. Sometimes they "*go fishing*", to see how much they can get away with. In my audit, most that was denied was contested

And all that was contested was won, with the help and advice of my accountant. (There was a lot of "fishing"…)

If you know the law, and if you have read the first two sections of this book, then you already know most of what you need.,.

So, you should be able to spot the parts that don't make sense. Note these down, as best you can, *before* seeing an accountant.

If you wait to the next phase (Appeal) before contacting an accountant you may make some errors in procedure in the Rebuttal.

Again, you should get help from an accountant at the Rebuttal stage to avoid mistakes. It could save you a lot of work later. Remember, you can do the grunge work yourself, but do get professional advice, so you know you are on the right track.

7.***Try to stay calm****. Certainly it is very stressful and you may be very angry.* But your accountant will usually help you through the mess and point out what you have to give them and what you can contest. That alone will help a lot.

8. **** Through the **whole process**, when replying to the tax department in the Rebuttal and the Appeal, *it is critical to be cool, calm, polite, diplomatic, respectful and accurate re the tax law.* This is *extremely* important!! **Do not express your opinion or ask questions**! The accountant can help with the tax law, but the tone and words you use are ultimately up to you. This is easier said than done, which is why you need the help of an accountant. She can help you learn how and then you can DIY with the knowledge you are on the right track.

There are many messes that artists can get themselves into, mostly because they are allowing their emotions to run away with them and they say unfortunate things. That can escalate something small into something much bigger, and make whoever they are dealing with at the tax department dig their heels in and perpetuate something that could have been resolved in a reasonable way much sooner.

Get advice on "safer" wording. Most disputes can be resolved amicably with a calm polite demeanor. Like they say, you catch more flies with honey than with vinegar.

You will have 90 days to do the *Rebuttal,* wherein you contest whatever you can, and concede whatever you have to, that you did not do correctly when you filed your returns.

9. ***The Appeal****:*   Several months after they get the Rebuttal, you will receive another mailing with their reply. You may get some of the *things that you contested, but there may be more things that they throw at you at this point.* This is where you go into the *Appeal process,* if all is not resolved. (They might not tell you that you can appeal !) At this stage, you definitely need an accountant, even if only for advice.

Do not DIY the Appeal*:* you *absolutely* need an accountant at this stage. You can write it if you want but have your accountant read it over to be sure you have the tax law correct and your language is suitable and not inflammatory.

At this point you have another *90 days to appeal.* There is a special form this time, on which you can give the name of your accountant. They will confer with your accountant, if needed, and your accountant can get some background on what actually happened which you would not be able to find out on your own. Your accountant knows people at the tax offices. Also your accountant can talk Tax Department "language".

A different "Tax Court" (an office, really) in a different city will be appointed to deal with the Appeal procedure. That is a good thing, especially if there is a lot being contested, as it allows you to have a fair hearing that is not biased in any way.

Several months later, you will receive a *final ruling*, and hopefully news that you will get all or part of your money back within a few more months.

Depending on how long the delays are between the various stages, the whole process can take a minimum of 1 year to 2 years. The average is 18 months. Do NOT try to hurry them up: that will only make matters worse. Now do you see why you pay what they say up front to stop the clock on interest building up? If you don't pay up front, the interest and penalties could add up to a big amount.

One thing that can make a big difference: In Canada we have something called the *"**Access To Information Act**",* which entitles individuals to find out what is in files on them.

You can apply for "*Access to Information*" on your tax file pertaining to the year in question. It takes about 6 weeks to come and will be a big box, including a lot of items copied several times, and some lines blacked out (redacted), but you never know, there could be a little gem in there, so look over it *very carefully*. Where you see numbers added up, add them up with a calculator. Don't assume they were done with a computer.

In one case there was a list of gross and net income numbers for 10 years. The gross was correct, but the net column was way, way off: They had not added in certain numbers, and came to the conclusion that the artist did not have a viable business. The correct total, of course, made a big difference, once the artist pointed out in the Appeal that "an arithmetic error in the addition" had been made (note the low key polite language).

Never assume that is accurate, and always double check the math, in case there is an error that might make a difference in your case.

10. *My experience:*   In my audit procedure, I had an advantage in that I know the tax law well, thanks to my Financial Planner background and all the

courses I had taken over the years and over 40+ years of DIY accounting wherein I have learned a lot.

Not being a push-over, I came back with chapter and verse all the way. All my replies (initial, Rebuttal, Appeal) were self-written, but there was help with some wording and points of law from my accountant on the Appeal.

(Again, however, it is better to bring an accountant into the picture at the Rebuttal stage) .

A small percentage of detail was conceded, including some errors on my part plus some tidbits on the advice of my accountant it is wise to "give some crumbs" and those were the ones they like, yet most points were contested and won .

In my case, if the whole thing had been done by an accountant instead of DIY with advice, it would have cost more than the amount contested, to fight.

Some artists cave in as it is not economically viable to fight, especially if they feel they need to have an accountant do all the work for them.

The problem with that is that if you cave in, you may be doing some things incorrectly ongoing and have a *worse mess later.* Also, if you cave in, it will be assumed that you agree you were *wrong/ guilty on everything and that would be on your record.*

So, ***fight for your rights*** (if you *are actually* in the right, of course). It is your democratic right to do so. With this book, plus some accountant advice, you should be able to do what I did: ***DIY with a side of advice.***

They say that a previous Auditor General was of the opinion that artists are "too small potatoes" to hassle, not worth the taxpayers dollar to chase, although there have been several cases of hassling, possibly aggravated by use of unfortunate language.

In my case, it cost the taxpayer many times more in manpower than what the Tax Department got out of the exercise.

Audit Summary:

What have you learned about audits?

1.There are many things that could trigger an audit

2. You have learned exactly what will happen if you get audited and what to do about it

3. You have specific legal rights in the audit process

4. You have learned exactly how and when to make use of an Accountant for your audit.

MY NOTES:

_____
_____
_____
_____
_____
_____
_____
_____
_____
_____
_____
_____
_____
_____
_____
_____
_____
_____
_____

****

PART IV

Epilogue :
Estate Planning
for Artists

****

Epilogue :

Estate Planning

for Artists

For all art media, it is important to remember that *keeping one's Will up to date is critical*. And for heaven's sake do not use one of those "will kits' !! Those are worse than useless for artists. They will cause more trouble than help and are only meant for the very simplest of situations. Artists of all types almost always have very complex estate situations compared to the general public.

Deemed Disposition:

It is important to note that everything the artist owns at death triggers a "deemed disposition" on the death of the artist . Deemed disposition means a deemed (hypothetical on paper) "sale" at fair market value based on one minute before the death of the artist. This automatically triggers tax on both the Provincial and Federal side on most items owned by the artist/deceased person. (It goes without saying that all of this deemed stuff also applies to the general population too.)

For visual artists, who are hit the hardest, every work of art including each and every original edition print, drawing/sketch have to be evaluated one by one by a professional art appraiser accredited in Ontario (if that is where the artist lives at the time of death). The equivalent applies to all other provinces as well.

So far, the other provinces of Canada are on the older method wherein the executor/trustee (usually a family member) can "appraise" the art even though they may have no training for that.

Needless to say, the method outside of Ontario can result is very different valuation, usually somewhat lower based on the artist's prices which may or may not be realistic or accurate.

The New Ontario Estate Law:

As of January 1, 2015, in Ontario, the new *Estate Administration Tax*.(aka Probate) requires only *accredited appraisers*, not family /friends, to do the appraising. Presumably these appraisals should be more "accurate". Such appraisals are NOT based on the prices of the art, but other criteria altogether. Normally they are based more on the value as per the Resale/After Market/Auction world including the condition, documentation (Authentication Certificate), archival aspects, quality, and salability at auction and have to be justifiable in tax court..

Families may be shocked to find that the prices their loved one set on the art may be very much lower than the standards of the appraisal world. Hence the tax may be considerably higher than the family might have expected. The appraisal process is laborious, detailed, and expensive (at the expense of the estate) . And of course the provincial appraisal sets up the federal valuation automatically.

One might assume that "potential" art which resides only on the computer, and may not ever see the light of day, does not "count". Fingers crossed on that. Also it is usually assumed that student work under instruction does not "count" as inventory, and is therefore not appraised. And work as an amateur in the visual artist's early years is usually taxed as Personal Use Property along with household goods, which results in lower tax federally.

Keep in mind that the provincial estate admin tax is at 1.5% while the federal tax will usually be at 50% by the time the whole estate is considered.

Yet the real kicker is that the provincial (Ontario) appraisal is due *90 days after the death of the artist!* Not much time to rush around doing all those estate things as well as the complex appraisal.

The federal side, however gives lots of time to finish the rest of the things one needs to do in settling the estate. It will take a minimum of 6 months to maximum of 16 months, depending on the exact date of death, since the two filing dates are April 30 and June 30. One can, of course file earlier than required, but there is no leeway to file late.

As you can imagine, the other provinces in Canada are keeping a close eye on how this new law will pan out in Ontario and whether it will prove to be the cash cow that Ontario expects it to be. If it works out as Ontario expects, don't be surprised if other provinces will follow suit in future years.

It took Ontario four years to work out the details, and we don't know yet how all this will work in practise. And of course there will be the attendant jump in federal tax on estate on the deemed valuation which in most cases will be higher than that resulting from self-appraisal .

As far as inventory is concerned, the effect of all this on musicians, writers and actors should be minimal (except musicians who own very valuable instruments).

However, I do note that in the list of taxable property in Ontario, is an item called "*intellectual property*". This will again hit the visual artists hard re copyright on their physical art. Here the more valuable the visual art is, the higher the value of the copyright.   Also best-selling /famous novelists, songwriters, and composers should take note re both copyright and trademarks. They say that in fact the valuation of intellectual property is a "shot in the dark", so keep fingers crossed on that one… Time will tell how this aspect of the new law will pan out.

And that big fly in the ointment is the provincial Ontario deadline: only three months from death to get everything appraised , reported and submitted. A huge task especially if the artist dies in old age and was prolific!

Contrary to common opinion most visual artists, even famous ones, build up a large inventory of unsold works, so the tax bill could be crippling to the estate. It would be not uncommon to owe tax in 6 or even 7 figures (on the Federal side)!

So what effect would this have on the beneficiary of the art and the estate as a whole? Often, even usually, the beneficiary of the visual art is also a main beneficiary of the estate as a whole. The tax on the estate must be paid before any of the estate is distributed. So tax first, and then the art is received.

It is not uncommon for estate sales and auctions to need to be held in order to raise money to pay the tax bill. Investments may need to be sold; the family home may need to be sacrificed.

This may put the beneficiary/family in difficult straits, especially if the assets are needed by the beneficiary. It is always best to name one beneficiary for the art: it is less complex that way. The sole beneficiary of the visual art is always free to "share" later since the tax has already been paid, so deemed disposition will not result in tax (x-x=0) .

"Rights or Things":

There is however one saving grace for the visual artist: a weird sounding thing called *"rights or things"*:

Normally *"rights or things"* are used only by farmers and fishermen. Most lawyers, even estate lawyers, know nothing of the use of *"rights or things"* by visual artists.

Some background to the use of *"rights or things"*: Visual artists have been allowed to claim their inventory at Zero officially since 1986. Actually everyone claimed at zero long before that but not legally.

Back in '86, artist Toni Onley was in receipt of a tax bill for his unsold inventory for $1,000,000. (Adjusted for inflation that works out to about $5,600,000 in today's dollars.) This was based on his unsold inventory of $2M.

A highly popular and best-selling artist, who sold a lot of works, he still had built up a huge inventory over time. He refused to pay. Being very media savvy, he called lots of media, notified the PM office (Pierre Elliott Trudeau was the PM), and proceeded to pile up his taxable inventory on a beach in Vancouver.

With everyone gathered holding their collective breaths, he threatened to light a match to his whole inventory before he would pay one cent of tax. Trudeau's staffer yelled "Wait.. wait! We'll do something" ... So everyone went home and next thing you know a tiny clause was stuffed into an Omnibus bill, giving artists the right to claim their inventory at zero during their lifetime. So there is officially no tax on unsold inventory for visual artists (includes both unincorporated and incorporated) during their lifetime, as that inventory is claimed as zero value ongoing..

So far so good, but every coin has 2 sides! The other side of the coin is the deemed disposition on death, at the current value, which of course includes inflation over time and the effect of the artist's CV/reputation as an artist.

So they had to add a little sentence to another Omnibus document (very hard to find and few know about it), which allows the named beneficiary of the visual artist, who has always claimed inventory at zero, to claim "*rights or things*" if they wish. Note there is just one beneficiary.

This means that the beneficiary can continue to value the inventory at zero for their lifetime. The use of "*rights or things*" is optional.

If you ever find yourself in a situation where "*rights or things*" could be useful for your beneficiary, please tell them about it, as it could make a huge difference in many circumstances.

The beneficiary would need to meet with an accountant who specializes in estates, as there are special forms to be filled out and only that type of accountant would have them. Your own accountant should be able to refer you on to the right kind of accountant, as they are rare and usually well known in the community.

If needed by the beneficiary, using *"rights or things"* would give more time to edit, edit, edit and auction, auction, auction to reduce the inventory and therefore tax to a dull roar, so to speak. The use of *"rights or things"* does not continue on to anyone else, only the first beneficiary named in the will who survives the visual artist so obviously time is of the essence.

However in some cases using *"rights or things"* is not the best way to go so talk this over thoroughly and consider all the angles. Once in the beneficiary is "in" the system, he or she cannot cancel, so it is a serious decision..

Use of Schedule A and B:

Copies of these should be kept in your Safe Deposit Box along with the Will, and important papers.

Applies to all artists and all who have a Will.

There are many things which are essential to notify your executor/trustee about but which would be awkward or too wordy to put into the Will proper. They would make the Will too lengthy and may also keep changing as time goes on, necessitating too many Will rewrites. These items could be written outside of the Will in what I call "*Schedule A*". Your lawyer may have a different name for them, but that does not change the purpose.

Here is a list of what you should have in your Schedule A and B, which may very well turn out to be longer than the Will itself.

Schedule A (for general assets):

1. Current *passwords* (keep this up to date and only keep the written version in your Safe Deposit Box, for safety)

2. Where The Safe Deposit Box is, including what is in your Safe Deposit Box, and where that SDB is (which bank, and the address.) The trustee will have to prove ID, and show a copy of the Will saying they are the trustee in order to access.

3. Details of specific bequests of certain treasured physical items for specific persons, including photos to help identification.

4. Recommended professionals including estate accountants, real estate personnel, estate lawyer.

5. Bank accounts, important assets, investments, credit cards

6. List of insurances (Life, House, Medical, etc.) with account numbers, phone contacts.

7. Current valuation of the principal residence, cottage, and any other real estate, including addresses. The family cottage, by the way, is included in "Personal Use Property" along with the cutlery, china, furniture, etc.

8. Approximate value of investments (stocks, mutual funds, RRSPs, etc.)

9. Inventory of collectibles (fine art, rare stamps and coins/bullion, antiques, valuable jewellery, etc.) These are "Listed Personal Property"..

10. Where valuables and important paperwork around the home are hidden.

Schedule B *(for your Business assets)*

1.   Physical assets of your business

2.   Where your business assets/art are situated (visual artists especially need to keep an up to date list of where their art is, since they tend to show in many places ongoing.)

3.   Inventory of the physical art (mostly visual art) which is subject to deemed: including small icons of the images, title, size, medium, etc. Be sure to keep this list up to date as you produce more art.

4.   Options and suggestions re owning and running of the business (for the beneficiary of the business), including options for "editing down" and auctioning of the art where appropriate.

5.   Explanation of *"rights or things"* if needed for the visual art of your estate and how/why to use it if needed.

As you can see the use of both Schedule A (for personal stuff) and Schedule B (for your business related stuff) will make the life of your Trustee a lot easier. Having been a Trustee myself 4 times now for family, I know that it is a huge and complex job and any help like the above would have been very welcome if I had had it.

It is a lot of work to figure out what you want in your Will and to do your Schedule A and B, but believe me your Trustee and beneficiaries will be very grateful you took the time to do it.

Postscript: The most famous example of an artist who neglected all this is Picasso who died without a Will. Today over forty years later his potential beneficiaries are still fighting over the estate and so far no money has gone to anyone except a team of lawyers who are doing very well indeed... Lesson learned ??

Use of Life Insurance:

Universal Life insurance costs more up front, but stays at same cost ongoing throughout your life, and hence seems cheap long term as you get old. Term insurance is cheap when young but gets very expensive as you age and gets cut off at 69 or 74 right when you need it most. You can use insurance to help pay the tax on the deemed on your art.

Estate Planning Summary

What have you learned about estates?

1. **You need an up to date Will.**
2. **There is a deemed disposition on everything , including your art, when you die.**
3. **Everything will need to be appraised by a professional.**
4. ***"Rights or Things"* can be valuable for some beneficiaries**
5. **Use of Schedule A and B will help your executor/trustee**
6. **Life insurance can be used to help with tax on deemed dispositions.**

MY NOTES:

_____

_____

_____

_____

_____

_____

_____

_____

_____

_____

_____

_____

_____

_____

_____

_____

_____

_____

Author BIO

Jessie Parker has an unusual background for writing this book. For more info , see her bio/cv on her art website:www.photobasedart.com

For now, in a nutshell:

Professional visual artist five decades in the Maritimes, Ontario and UK; art teacher many years ; public speaker at National Gallery of Canadas; professional photographer 40+years, including for National Museums. *Most pertinent*: Certified Financial Planner seven years; many accounting courses and own accounting 40+ years; successful audit, many seminars on accounting, tax for artists.